Memoirs of a Warsaw Ghetto Fighter

Memoirs of a Warsaw Ghetto Fighter

Kazik (Simha Rotem)

Translated from the Hebrew and edited
by Barbara Harshav

Yale University Press   New Haven and London

Set in Trump type by Rainsford Type, Danbury,
Connecticut.
Printed in the United States of America by Vail-
Ballou Press, Binghamton, New York.

ISBN 0-300-09376-4 (pbk.: alk. paper)
Library of Congress Control Number: 2001094275
A catalogue record for this book is available from
the British Library.

10 9 8 7 6 5 4 3 2

Contents

Introduction

In September 1939, when the Germans invaded Poland and started World War II, there were some 360,000 Jews in Warsaw, about 30 percent of the total population of the capital. The interwar period had been marked by an increase in political activity among Jews, resulting in a proliferation of parties and movements, ranging from assimilationists to Zionists (of various kinds) to socialists (of various stripes) to the entire gamut of religious orthodoxy; and the capital with its large Jewish population naturally became the center for these groups. In addition, Warsaw spawned an active Jewish cultural life, comprising schools, theaters, journalism, and the arts. In short, despite an upsurge in home-grown Polish anti-Semitism in the 1930s, Jewish life in Warsaw was flourishing when the Nazi invasion and subsequent occupation put an end to that civilization.

Although the actual Ghetto was not officially established until September 1940, Jews had already been excluded from the life of the city and deprived of their livelihoods and businesses. They were subject to brutal roundups for forced labor, their food rations were cut, and they were prey to the periodic violence of both Poles and Nazi Germans. Conditions became even worse after the Ghetto was sealed off with a ten-foot wall on November 15, 1940.

This area of 3.5 square miles (2.4 percent of the area of Warsaw) initially contained one-third of the city's inhabitants. The Ghetto population was further increased by refugees from the surrounding area, reaching a peak of 445,000 in March 1941. With scant food, heating materials, and medical facilities and supplies, the mortality rate in the Ghetto soared. Between January 1941 and May 1942, some 66,000 people died of starvation and the diseases associated with it, as well as under the harsh conditions of deportation and labor camps.

But even this high rate of attrition did not satisfy the Nazis. On January 20, 1942, at the Wannsee Conference in Berlin, the "Final Solution" was officially adopted. In July and August of that year, 300,000 Warsaw Jews were rounded up and deported, primarily to the death camp of Treblinka, where most of them were murdered.

It was during this so-called Great Aktsia that the Jewish Fighting Organization (known by its Polish initials, ZOB) was established; its objective was to mount an armed resistance against the Nazi death machine. To appreciate the magnitude of this undertaking, it is necessary to recall that the organization consisted almost entirely of young men and women (the oldest were in their late twenties; most were between 18 and 21) who had virtually no weapons, no influence, no money, and no experience in warfare. All they had were a remarkable strength of will, tremendous reserves of intelligence and courage, and amazing talents for initiative and innovation.

Armed with these qualities and little else, the young Jewish fighters fiercely resisted the Nazi attempt to liquidate the Warsaw Ghetto, first on January 18 and later on April 19, 1943. The Germans had planned to complete the operation in three days, but the five hundred members of the ZOB forces—fighting with a few pistols and rifles, and homemade Molotov cocktails and bombs—managed to hold out for almost a month. In the end, when the battle was lost, most of the remaining fighters committed suicide in the famous command bunker at Mila 18. A handful survived and were led through the sewers to the "Aryan side" of the city by the nineteen-year-old Kazik. This dramatic episode was recounted by Kazik many years later and forms the conclusion of Claude Lanzmann's film *Shoah*.

Now a new stage of operations began for the ZOB. Even

though Warsaw was officially *Judenrein* ("cleansed" of its Jews), perhaps 20,000 Jews remained in hiding in the city and its environs. Instead of preparing for armed conflict with the Nazis, the Fighting Organization now shifted to a rescue and support force. It received monies from Jewish organizations through the Polish underground, with which it maintained some 3,000 Jews.[1] This enormous effort required a network of couriers to find apartments for the Jews, to fill their various requirements, such as providing doctors, and to bring them money and other material assistance.

Just as preparing for armed resistance in the Ghetto had demanded extraordinary courage and intelligence and entailed grave dangers, so did the rescue operation on the Aryan side. Except for Kazik, all the couriers were women (who could not be identified as easily as the Jewish men). Most of them were young, looked "good"—that is, like Aryan Poles—and spoke perfect Polish. And they put their lives at constant risk.

Finally, in August 1944, when the Polish Uprising erupted in Warsaw, the ZOB once again entered the fighting, this time in a special unit (led by Zuckerman) within the Polish forces. That uprising, too, failed spectacularly, and the Nazis exacted a severe punishment; estimates of those killed are as high as 150,000, and much of the city was destroyed as well.[2]

When the liberation finally came, it was accompanied by a sense of desolation and confusion among those Jews who had survived. Learning of the almost total destruction of their people, they had little inclination to rejoice at their freedom. Moreover, even after the war the Jews in Poland continued

1. According to Yitzhak Zuckerman, who was then the leader of ZOB, the organization took responsibility for about 3,000 of the roughly 20,000 Jews hiding in and around Warsaw (Zuckerman 1993: 449).

2. See Zuckerman 1993: 525.

to suffer persecution, this time at the hands of the Poles. The most dramatic example was the pogrom in Kielce in 1946, where forty-two Jews were killed and several others wounded.

For some of the former fighters, like Yitzhak Zuckerman, the only answer to the plight of the remnant of European Jewry was immediate immigration to Palestine. Another group, led by Abba Kovner, commander of the Vilna partisans, wanted to remain temporarily in Europe to wreak vengeance on the Germans for the murder of the Jews. Kazik joined the vengeance group, whose story has yet to be told. In June 1946 he immigrated illegally to Palestine, where he settled into private life—unlike many of his former comrades in arms, who led more public careers. Forty years after the events, Simha Rotem/Kazik wrote these memoirs.
—Barbara Harshav

Editor's Note

Except for note 80, I have supplied all the annotations, drawing from the works listed in the References as well as from the *Encylopaedia Judaica*.

Preface

In the spring of 1944 a small group of Jewish Fighting Organization (ZOB) members gathered in an apartment hideout on the Aryan side of Warsaw, at Panska Street 5, to record our experiences during the war since 1939.[1]

Some had been in permanent hiding in the apartment; others, who had come from "outside," were surviving leaders of the organization and former Jewish leaders in Poland. At that time—between the Warsaw Ghetto Uprising (April–May 1943) and the Polish Uprising (August 1944)—one of the most important activities of the ZOB was documentation. Its leaders had a strong sense of history and felt they were the last remaining Jews. Hence they assumed the responsibility to preserve, and to tell, the story of Polish Jewry in the "days of destruction and revolt."[2] Many accounts were written in that ZOB apartment; Yitzhak Zuckerman, alias "Antek," was the group's life force, devoted to collating the accounts.[3]

I was eight or nine years younger than Antek, with whom I worked on the Aryan side. When you're in your twenties, that's a big age difference. I didn't share his political contacts and ties with the various movements, but I did participate in

1. The Zydowska Organizacja Bojowa (ZOB), or Jewish Fighting Organization, was founded in the Warsaw Ghetto in August 1942. The "Aryan side" of Warsaw was the part of the city outside of the Ghetto reserved for the non-Jewish population. By 1944 the Ghetto had been destroyed.

2. This is the title of Zivia Lubetkin's memoirs (Lubetkin 1981).

3. Yitzhak Zuckerman (1915–1981), known as Antek, was born in Vilna. Active in the halutz movement and leader of the ZOB in Warsaw, he immigrated to Israel after the war and was one of the founders of Kibbutz Lohamei Ha-Gettaot (the Ghetto Fighters' Kibbutz). See his memoirs (Zuckerman 1993).

the staff discussions concerning ZOB operations. Frankly, I wasn't interested in what traces the movement or any individual would leave behind in history; I wanted to act. I didn't take part in the debates about what would or would not be written. My activity was centered outside the apartment—on the roads and underground. But Antek kept after me to write my memoirs as a fighter. So, in the spring of 1944, I too sat down at Panska 5 and wrote, in Polish, a kind of retrospective diary. I normally spoke Polish, although at home we also spoke Yiddish. My Polish was popular Polish, unlike the language of the Jewish intelligentsia.

In 1946, when I arrived in Palestine, Melekh Neustadt, who was preparing his book *Destruction and Uprising of the Jews of Warsaw*, called me in and showed me a Hebrew translation of my account, which he was publishing under the title *Diary of a Fighter*; since then the diary has been reprinted in a number of books and translated into several languages.[4] It describes events I participated in, from the first day of the uprising in the Warsaw Ghetto to the exodus of the group of fighters from the Ghetto through the sewers of Prosta Street. But I kept most of the story to myself, although as time passed Antek continued to urge me to write my memoirs. I didn't give in until 1981, when I came to Kibbutz Lohamei Ha-Gettaot and started writing. But it didn't work; so Antek asked Tzvika Dror, a member of the kibbutz, to write down what I dictated. That wasn't easy, since I'm not much of a talker. Antek died in 1981 and, because of the obligation I feel toward him, I continued to tell the tale.

Now I live in Jerusalem with my wife, Gina, and my children, Itai and Eyal. I've never told them these things in sequence either. I tell things as I normally speak, in the every-

4. A translation of this text is in the Appendix. Neustadt's book was published in Palestine in 1947.

day language I use at home, at work, and with my friends. I prefer to remain Kazik in writing too.

I tell only what I remember, without reservation and without considering my personal image or the impression I made on history. I want to convey things as I saw them then—and as I see them now—in my own way; and I take full responsibility for what is written here. Now and then the reader will find that the tale is not consecutive, since there are some blanks in my memory. I didn't want to "restore" memories and preferred to leave the "holes." I hope this will not make it hard for the reader to find his way around in this account.

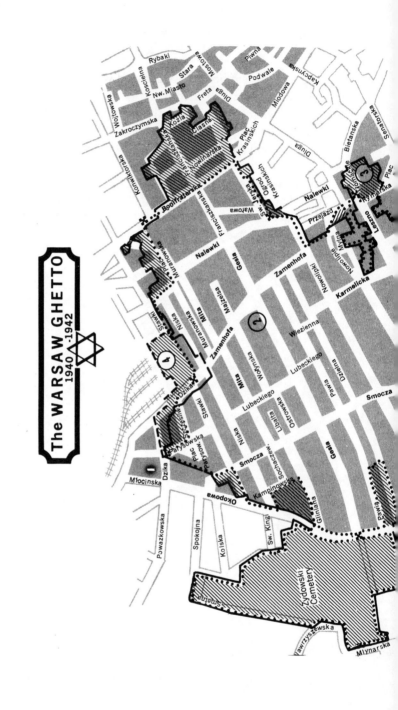

The WARSAW GHETTO
1940 -1942

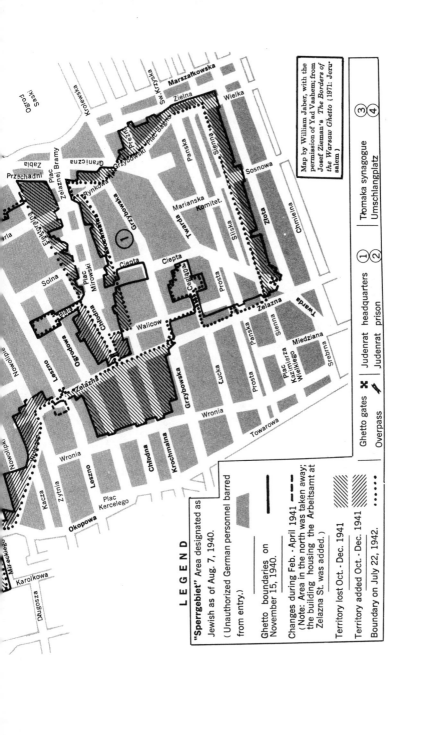

LEGEND

"Sperrgebiet" Area designated as Jewish as of Aug. 7, 1940.
(Unauthorized German personnel barred from entry.)

Ghetto boundaries on November 15, 1940.

Changes during Feb.-April 1941
(Note: Area in the north was taken away; the building housing the Arbeitsamt at Zelazna St. was added.)

Territory lost Oct.-Dec. 1941

Territory added Oct.-Dec. 1941

Boundary on July 22, 1942.

Ghetto gates ✗

Overpass ⟋

Judenrat headquarters ①

Judenrat prison ②

Tłomaka synagogue ③

Umschlangplatz ④

Map by William Jaber, with the permission of Yad Vashem; from Josef Zieman's *The Borders of the Warsaw Ghetto* (1971: Jerusalem.)

1 Before: Son of a Warsaw Family

Both sides of my family are Warsaw Jews. I was born in Czerniaków, a suburb of Warsaw, and spent my childhood there. My mother's parents, Grandfather Yakov Minski and Grandmother Sara (née Poznanski), also lived in Czerniaków with their four daughters and their families. When they all assembled, there was quite a tumult.

My parents were Miriam and Zvi Ratheiser. I was the oldest of four children. Israel, Dina, and Raya came after me. Only two of us survived the war—my sister Raya, who also lives in Israel, and I.

In my childhood I was close to each of my grandfathers in a special way. I was close to Grandfather Yakov because of his peasant nature and because it was fun to work with him. He was a hearty man, both physically and emotionally; his thinking was simple and his speech plain, and he had no interest in philosophy. He got up early in the morning and worked long and hard in villages about fifteen miles from his home. (I remember the name of only one of them—Siekierki.) He would buy fruit when it was still on the trees; when it ripened, he would hire laborers to pick it. Some of the fruit he stored to sell later, and some he sold immediately. The harvest season came during summer vacation from school. I loved to help drag the cases of fruit—apples, pears, cherries. A storehouse for the fruit was connected to our house, and there was a stable in the yard.

Grandfather Yakov used to take me with him in a horse-drawn cart. When we met a peasant on the way, we would get out of the cart and all of us would greet each other. The peasants called Grandfather "Mr. Yankl." They liked and trusted him—his word was his bond and he always kept his

1

promise. He would introduce me as "my grandson Shimek" (my nickname in the family). The Gentile neighbors used to say I was "like my grandfather," not like most other Jews. Aside from his beard, nothing marked Grandfather as a Jew, neither his speech, nor his way of life, nor his gestures. He looked just like a Polish peasant. My other grandfather, however, my father's father, was altogether different. Even eating was different in the homes of my two grandfathers.

Siekierki was a small village of brick huts with thatched roofs; next to every hut were a barn and a shed, along with a cellar for storing potatoes and onions for the year; outside was a well. Some of the village houses had electricity. Houses stood about a hundred feet apart and barnyards were fenced with low hedges, more as a symbol of property lines than to keep anybody out. At least one dog roamed every yard.

When Grandfather Yakov and I came to the village, we would enter a peasant hut where we were welcomed with respect and genuine warmth. I felt comfortable with the peasants. Grandfather spoke spicy Polish, without any Jewish slang or idiom.

My father's parents, Grandfather Shmuel—called "Der shvartser Shmuel" (Black Samuel)—and Grandmother Sara, lived nearby. My father was one of nine sons. For his livelihood Grandfather Shmuel worked at a business he had set up in Grandfather Yakov's house; "for his soul" he served as the cantor and treasurer of the synagogue. But he did read a "liberal" newspaper, including the serial novel in it, which was intended primarily for Jewish women. When my uncle Eliahu asked him how he could read "novels," he replied: "It's good to know everything." My relations with Grandfather Shmuel were intellectual; he helped me with my studies, especially arithmetic, and thanks to him I had no trouble solving problems.

Relations between the two sides of the family were good. We lived nearby and the children played together. My father had a grandmother in the suburb of Powisle on the outskirts of Warsaw, which the Jews considered the "underworld" suburb. This grandmother, almost the only Jew in a Gentile area, kept a tavern there. Drunkards haggling and quarreling were an everyday sight. The ambulance visited the tavern frequently, and so did the police. Naturally, Saturday and Sunday were particularly rowdy, but that doesn't mean that an intellectual atmosphere prevailed there on weekdays. When I came with my father, his grandmother would ask me: "You don't want any cake, do you?" I quickly understood what I was supposed to reply, and there are no tasty cakes from my greatgrandmother's house in my memory.

My father, a bearded Jew, had the honor of standing at the Ark of the Covenant on the Days of Awe. He was a Hasid, while his father, Shmuel, was a Misnaged.[1] I remember the excitement we felt when we went to Rebbe Kalonymus Shapiro of Piaseczno. Throughout the war, including the Ghetto period, he gave a sermon every week. In his will he requested that his sermons (which were written down) be published in Eretz Israel, and his nephew in Jerusalem found and published them. When oppression intensified and it was hard for Jews to move around in public (I was still a child then), Father sent me on a few errands to the rebbe, to give him money Father had collected for him or had contributed himself. Sometimes I went to the rebbe to ask a question and he would welcome me immediately, which was considered unusual.

We lived in a working-class quarter where there weren't many Jewish families. In our neighborhood Sunday was a "happy" time—drunkards rolled around in the street, there were squabbles and fistfights, the air was filled with the sing-

---

1. Beginning in the late eighteenth century, there was severe opposition between the populist Hasidic sects, primarily based in central and eastern Poland among the poor and uneducated Jews, and the rationalist Misnaged faction, centered in Lithuania.

ing and shouts of sots. There were few Jewish children my age in the neighborhood, so I played mostly with Gentile children who came to my house. We'd play soccer, go down to the Wisla River and enjoy the fresh air, swim, and row. Later, when I went to the Jewish school, the Gentile children used to tease the Jewish children on their way to and from school, so we would walk in a group and felt safer. We didn't run away from Gentile hoodlums but fought back with blows and stones. Once I was attacked with a knife, but somehow it just grazed my head and merely scratched me. Even as a child I was never one to run away.

Our apartment, at Nowosielecka Street 8, had only two rooms and a kitchen. It was in a big four-storey building whose four wings surrounded a courtyard. The building was inhabited mainly by Poles; there were only two Jewish families, my Grandfather Shmuel's and ours.

In 1934 we moved to Podchorazych Street 24. Here too we lived with the family clan, but this apartment was a little roomier. My parents employed a cleaning woman (a *shikse*)— a sign of upward mobility and an improved economic situation.[2] They made their living running a store that sold paint, kerosene, building materials, and haberdashery. Ninety-nine percent of their customers were Poles, who got along well with my parents, especially my mother, who was pretty and known for her sincerity and warmth. The Poles used to say she didn't look Jewish and would ask: "How come you married a Jew?"

In the courtyard of the house I grew my own little garden, including flowers called *maciejka,* which had a very special fragrance. These flowers opened in the afternoon, emitting their delicate aroma. A few years ago the scent rose in my memory, and I asked some friends in Poland to send me maciejka seeds; but my attempts to plant them in my Jerusalem

2. A *shikse* was a Gentile, usually lower-class, girl.

garden didn't work out. I am left with only the memory of the scent.

My sister Raya was born in the house on Podchorazych Street. When Mother went into labor, I was sent to fetch the Polish midwife. I was at home when my sister was born, and perhaps that is why I felt especially close to her and would take her for walks when she was little.

I started my formal schooling in the *heder*, where I learned *Humash* and prayers.[3] But I soon quarreled with the teacher and ran away from the heder. The teacher, who felt responsible, sent some children to look for me and bring me back. When they followed me to my street, I sicked my Polish friends on them. The Poles took the opportunity to beat up the Jewish children and chased them back to their heder.

I attended a grammar school run by the Jewish community organization. It was considered an official state school, except that it was closed on Saturday and, along with general subjects, we studied Hebrew once a week. The school was modern both in its teaching methods and in its structure, since it was coeducational. I was a good student. I loved math and was thrilled when the teacher called me to the blackboard to explain complicated problems to the class. There were a lot of nice, pretty girls in school who, to my delight, lived far away, so I often had a chance to walk them partway home.

Approaching bar mitzvah, in 1937, I insisted that my father provide me with the traditional Hasidic attire. Perhaps I was influenced by religious friends. My father granted my wish and I entered my bar mitzvah year in black attire, with *arbe'kanfes*.[4] After the bar mitzvah ceremony, I no longer needed those clothes.

3. A *heder* is a Jewish elementary school, conducted in small classes at the teacher's home. *Humash* refers to the Pentateuch, or Five Books of Moses.

4. An *arbe'kanfes* is a sleeveless undershirt with four fringed corners worn by orthodox Jews.

I completed seven grades in that school.

At the same time, when I was about twelve (at any rate, before my bar mitzvah), I started attending meetings of the pioneer youth movement Ha-No'ar Ha-Zioni (Zionist Youth). When I went to summer camp, my father made sure I took my *tefillin*, but I didn't touch them the whole time I was there.[5] That was the only time I attended Ha-No'ar Ha-Zioni summer camp, where we participated in scouting, hikes, camping, group singing, and lectures on the Zionist movement and Eretz Israel.

When one of my friends and his family, the Steins, immigrated to Eretz Israel in 1938, it made a great impression on us. The letters and pictures he sent me right up to the outbreak of the war added a note of reality to my desire to immigrate to Eretz Israel.

A year before the war, I went to study at the vocational high school of the Jewish community organization at Grzybowska Street 26.

The Germans Occupy Warsaw: Trapped in the Rubble

On the day the war began I was in the city.[6] I might have been on my way to school when suddenly we heard the noise of airplanes. Some people said the city was being bombed; others said the planes were taking part in Polish air force maneuvers. Soon it became obvious that German airplanes were attacking and that war had broken out.

Even in those first days, it was hard for people to get food. Tunnels were dug and barricades were built. Bedraggled soldiers, survivors of units on the collapsing front, began to appear in the streets. The situation deteriorated from one day

5. *Tefellin:* two black leather boxes containing scriptural passages which are bound by black leather straps to the head and the left arm; worn at daily prayer by pious Jews.

6. Sept. 1, 1939.

to the next, and panic and depression increased. My parents decided to leave our house in the Polish area and move to a Jewish neighborhood. It was hard to get bread, so every day I would go back to our former residence, where a *Volksdeutsch* (a Polish citizen of German origin) was living. He was a friend of my father's and provided us with unlimited quantities of bread. As the bombings intensified, it was often hard for me to recognize a place I had passed the day before because rows of houses had turned into heaps of ruins. The Jewish quarter and the center of the city were especially damaged, and so my parents decided to return to our old house, hoping it would be quieter. But the evil quickly reached us there too, and our house was hit by a bomb the day after Yom Kippur.[7]

If I'm not mistaken, this occurred three days before the surrender of Warsaw. Three half-ton bombs (as I was later told) damaged the house and one made a direct hit, killing and wounding many residents, including Grandfather and Grandmother (my mother's parents), my aunt Hannah (my mother's sister), my aunt Zissl's husband, one cousin, and my brother Israel, aged fourteen. I was seriously wounded. When I came to, I found myself trapped in the rubble: my neck was caught in a tangle of lines, apparently electrical cords. I started considering how to get out, but I acted cautiously for fear of electrocuting myself; I moved the lines with leather gloves I happened to have with me. A stick torn off one of the beams by a blast was stuck in my neck, a "thorn" in my neck, piercing my windpipe. It was hard to breathe; I felt I was choking. Nevertheless, I managed to pull the stick out without losing too much blood.

I lay among the ruins, trapped to the waist. With great effort I managed to get my legs out of the debris. The German positions were about five hundred meters away, and when I got out, I saw that our house had been completely destroyed;

7. I.e., Sept. 24.

there were no signs of life. I reached the shelter in the house next door, where I found my parents and my two sisters. Obviously, the other members of the family had all been killed. My uncle Moyshe Krengel, who lived in our house, had been away during the bombing. When he came home, he pointed to me and said, "Who's that?" His question made me realize that I was unrecognizable, since my face was scratched and covered with a layer of clotted blood.

There was no first-aid in the area, and Red Cross nurses didn't arrive until several hours later. They told me that one nurse had been killed on the way. I was bandaged and about to be taken to the hospital. The nurses asked for volunteers to carry my stretcher. A volunteer was finally found, but as soon as we left a salvo was fired at us from the German positions on the outskirts of the city. Especially heavy fire was aimed at this very area. My escorts left me on the stretcher and ran for cover. This happened several times until I was finally taken to a police station, where I was put on a horse-drawn wagon about to leave for an assembly point of wounded people, which was even closer to the front. On the way we saw destroyed houses and many empty spaces. A Polish soldier was driving the wagon. Before we reached our destination, there was more heavy fire, and the soldier kept abandoning me and hiding. Finally, taking advantage of a brief lull in the fighting, he burst out of hiding and brought me to the place where dozens of wounded were lying. Unfortunately, no one was there to tend to the wounded, who lay without food or care for about twenty-four hours. A bomb exploding nearby jolted us onto our feet. I, who couldn't move, suddenly seemed to sprout wings, and in a few seconds I was in the street. I tried to find my way back to the shelter where my parents were, but it was hard to walk and at each step I leaned against the walls. Fortunately, I came upon my classmate Arye Krim, who carried me to the shelter on his back.

A day or two later, Warsaw surrendered and the German army took control of the city.

I was terribly curious to see the Germans enter Warsaw and I asked to be taken outside. Units of the Polish army and Polish guards returning from the front were busy taking down the barricades and filling in excavations so the German regiments could parade through the streets of the capital. The picture is still engraved in my memory: perfect order, motorcycles, riders on their horses, steel helmets. I was depressed and scared.

My parents took me to the hospital as soon as they could. I looked awful. Several fragments of shrapnel were found in my body, but they decided not to operate because conditions in the hospital were so bad. The shrapnel is still stuck there today.

Because of the way the members of my family had been killed, they couldn't have a proper Jewish burial, so they were buried in a makeshift grave in the courtyard of the house. Right after the cease-fire, when Poland surrendered, their bodies were taken to the Jewish cemetery in the city. The disinterment shocked me. For the first time in my life I saw a person who had been killed. I caught sight of a hand separated from a body and was told it was my brother's hand; it was buried next to his grave.

The day after the Germans entered, I saw Jews picked up in the street for forced labor. These were mostly Jews who were easily identifiable, that is, religious Jews. I felt a dull sense of impending disaster, something I couldn't explain. The Germans were mocking the Jews, treating them cruelly, knocking their hats off, pushing and hitting them. A few days later things apparently settled down; my parents' store reopened, trading, buying and selling—business as usual. September passed, October; November came. A *Treuhänder* (a trustee appointed by the Germans, generally a Volksdeutsch) appeared on the scene and our store was transferred to his management, in fact to his ownership. The Germans searched from house to house, from apartment to apartment, and naturally did not neglect the Jews. Under the pretext of looking for weapons, they searched our house thoroughly, even rummaging in the oven.

Morale was low. Many Jews organized in small groups, planning to go east, cross the River Bug, and get to the Russian-occupied zone.[8] One of them was my cousin Simha, the son of Hannah and Moyshe Krengel, who was two or three years older than me. I wanted to go with him but my parents wouldn't let me, so I stayed. We got one message and then lost track of him. I don't know what became of him. I urged my parents, especially Father, to let me go to the Soviets, but to no avail. Once I did seem to convince Father, but the issue kept getting postponed. Meanwhile, refugees began returning from the Soviet zone bearing bad news, which didn't encourage moving there.

Before the establishment of the Ghetto and the confiscation of the shops, life was more or less bearable under the Nazis, even though the first decrees were being issued here and there: an obligation to appear for forced labor, a ban on Jews riding on trams or buses with Poles (separate seats were set aside for them), a law forbidding kosher slaughter. Jews suffered more discrimination than Poles, which created an atmosphere of collaboration between the Polish population and the occupation authorities. This was especially manifest in the Polish practice of locating and identifying Jews and turning them over to the Germans. The Germans picked out some Jews by their appearance, especially by their clothing and beards, but they had trouble identifying others. The

8. According to a secret protocol of the Molotov-Ribbentrop Pact, signed on Aug. 23, 1939, Poland was divided between Germany and the Soviet Union.

Poles, who knew the Jews better, volunteered to find them and hand them over to the authorities.

The situation deteriorated. The illegal trade in food began to flourish right after the Germans introduced rationing. Basic foods became rarities, but you could usually still get them for a high price in the villages. If you managed to smuggle your wares (sausages, potatoes, eggs, cheese) into the city, you could make a lot of money. I decided to do something to provide food for my family; I went to the villages several times and brought home enough food to last a few weeks. If you were lucky on the train or the road—and if the Germans didn't search your bags—you succeeded. If you weren't lucky and got caught, the food was confiscated and you got beaten. Even at this stage, in trips to the villages, I looked like a Polish Christian. I was fifteen years old and looked just like a Gentile.

In the Ghetto

Announcement boards in the streets of Warsaw displayed notices in German and Polish addressed to the Jewish population. They were also published in the Polish newspapers under German control. The notices decreed that all Jews had to move to specific streets; by a certain date there would not be a single Jew left outside the Ghetto. My parents found an apartment at Swietojerska Street 34, which consisted of one small, dark room. We were imprisoned in the Ghetto, unable to go in or out except with a pass issued to those working outside on a recommendation from their employer; and we ventured out only in groups.

At first the Germans weren't strict and even allowed you to come into the Ghetto if you claimed you had lost your group or something like that. But going out—that was much harder. One day a decree was issued that all Jews aged sixteen to sixty had to register at the Judenrat, where they were divided into groups for jobs outside the Ghetto.[9] Usually there were no searches when you left, but when you returned there were searches at the gate, especially for food. Sometimes the guards would only take the food for themselves and wouldn't beat the "smugglers." Guard duty at the gate was handled by German gendarmes and Polish police, assisted by the Jewish police.

After our family had been crowded together for months in the small room, my parents managed to rent a big apartment, which looked like a palace compared with the other place. It was on the fourth floor, whereas the dark little room had been on the ground floor.

Even in those days there were signs of malnutrition. Hungry people wandered around the Ghetto. Rations were substandard. You couldn't live on them, and those who had to make do with them were doomed to a slow death. Contagious diseases soon began spreading in the Ghetto, especially typhus. People swollen with hunger were seen in the streets, rummaging through garbage cans and searching for scraps of food. Corpses were scattered about before being picked up in wheelbarrows going through the Ghetto and taken to the cemetery. These sights became routine; we started getting used to them and even grew indifferent.

To escape from hunger, my family started doing what others did: selling everything we had on the flourishing black market. Gangs of smugglers, especially youths, went into that business, although it entailed mortal danger. They banded together with groups outside the Ghetto, who threw them food over the wall. The Germans would open fire whenever they came on the smugglers, but hunger was oppressive and people took risks.

I tried my hand at smuggling a few times. My parents op-

9. The Judenrat was the Jewish council appointed by the Nazis to administer the Ghetto under the control of the occupiers.

posed it for fear I would get hurt, but when hunger intensified at home, no one could stop me. Apparently I was rather successful. Friends and relatives used to come to us for a bowl of soup, a sign that there was at least some food in our house. My mother, who looked like a Gentile, contributed the most to the household larder. She would go out to her acquaintances on the Aryan side and bring back various items of food.

Interlude in Klwów

I was sixteen and had to go to work. Briefly, even before the Ghetto was established, I had been sent to work in an apartment where some SS officers lived—a big, beautiful house, since SS officers didn't take simple houses. Our employers were the officers' wives or housekeepers. I worked at gardening, washing floors, cleaning. Part of our work was to bring furniture from the houses of expelled Jews. The furniture was transferred to the SS offices and other institutions. There was an advantage to this work: we got a special work card, which was no small thing. In those days I would come to the gathering place of my group in the morning and "our" German would take us to our destination. Since I didn't work every day, I exchanged my free days with Father or some other relative; I also went out from time to time as a substitute for one of the forced laborers who paid me for it. My parents didn't like this; they were scared of what might happen and, despite the advantages my work brought, they looked for something else for me.

Some of our relatives lived in a village, and it was mainly my mother who urged me to go there. Both she and my father thought that instead of wandering around the Ghetto exposed to danger, and without going to school, I would do better to try my luck in Klwów, not far from the district capital of Radom. Throughout the war I neither wore an armband outside the Ghetto nor sewed a yellow triangle on my clothes.

So I could take the train to the station closest to my destination, ten kilometers from Klwów, and walk there through
a thick forest, following a dirt path.

After I reached the tiny village, I had no trouble finding
my relatives. I asked them, as locals, to help me find work
with one of the peasants. My relatives were religious Jews
and didn't like the idea of a Jew working for a Gentile. But
since I insisted, they went to the peasants' houses and found
someone who agreed to hire me. The peasant knew that my
relatives were Jews and concluded that I was a Jew too. Nevertheless, I was hired to herd the cows even though Jews usually didn't do such work. No Germans were stationed in the
village, but now and then a German reconnaissance unit
would visit the area and go away.

I lived with my relatives. Early in the morning I would go to
the peasant's house, where I ate my fill of bread, potatoes, and
lard and drank milk. The wife cooked potatoes in a big pot and
stirred in lumps of fat. That was 1942, when my parents and
sisters lived in a Ghetto that was suffering from hunger and epidemics. There were five or six cows in the barn. I would take
them out to the pasture and stay there all morning and afternoon, almost until early evening. I had to bring the cows back
to the barn only for milking. It was summer. I'd lie in the
meadow, with the summer sky above me—all day long. I had
to bring the cows back to the barn only for milking. I'd lie in
the meadow for hours, staring at the sky, listening to the birds
singing. In the evening I'd return to my relatives' house to
sleep. But I was uneasy, haunted by the idea that people in the
Ghetto were suffering from hunger and disease while I lay between the green grass and the blue sky.

Through the entire summer of 1942, including the Great
Aktsia, I was in the village and had no contact with my parents.[10] From the day I left the city I hadn't heard anything

10. *Aktsia* refers to the brutal and violent roundup and deporta-

from them, not even a note. They didn't know anything about me either. For about half a year—until August 1942—I lived like a village boy, far from the distress my people were suffering. At that period, about 350,000 Jews were expelled from the Ghetto "for resettlement" and taken, as we later learned, to the death camps.

One day, the Germans decided to establish a ghetto even in that miserable village. The Jews were told that they were forbidden to leave a fenced-in area. No more than twenty Jewish families lived in the village, which consisted of one "main" street and a few meandering paths. In that village, for the first time in my life, I saw human beings killed. I saw a German kill a Jew in cold blood in broad daylight. German cavalry going through the place came on an old Jew standing behind a silo, urinating. They told him to come to them, and when he turned toward them, they shouted savagely: "You were outside the area!"—a capital crime. Meanwhile, the chairman of the local Judenrat arrived and begged them to spare the Jew's life. The Germans didn't answer. One of them aimed his rifle at the Jew. The Judenrat chairman gathered his strength and pushed the rifle aside; the German aimed again and shot. The old Jew fell, rolling in his own blood. I stood a few meters away from them. Until that moment I had not felt palpable danger from the Germans. The cavalry unit rode off, as if nothing had happened.

Return to Warsaw

Some time later I decided to return to Warsaw. I made my way as a Christian. Before I left the village, I bought a docu-

---

tion of Jews to concentration camps or to death. The Great Aktsia in the Warsaw Ghetto lasted six weeks between July and September 1942, when the Germans deported approximately 350,000 Jews, mostly to the death camp of Treblinka.

ment testifying that I was a Polish Christian. When I arrived in Warsaw, I learned that my parents had moved to a farm in Czerniaków.[11] During the great expulsion from the Warsaw Ghetto to the death camp of Treblinka in 1942, this farm was an isolated island, a workplace recognized by the German authorities. Miraculously, scores of young Zionist halutzim and ordinary Jews lived in a cooperative working at various jobs to support the farm and themselves. This state of affairs continued almost to the end of 1942. I went to the farm even though I wasn't on the list of workers. My father was working as a guard in the fields, and until they snuck my name on the list, I hid in his guard hut. Most of the Jewish workers were members of the Dror movement, but there were also a few families, including mine.[12] I heard for the first time about what had happened in the Ghetto and about the big expulsion. Later I became a blacksmith's apprentice and worked in the blacksmith shop for a few weeks.

I lived with my parents at the Czerniaków farm in a tent we put up in the field. The temperature was below zero centigrade. The Wisla River was nearby, and one day a Polish boy came by and taunted me: "Yid, you wouldn't dare go swimming in the river!" I taunted him back: "You won't!" To "show him," I undressed and went straight into the water. What can I say? I almost froze, while the *sheygets* didn't go in.[13] Plunging into the freezing water, I felt as if I were taking revenge on him.

Among the Zionist halutzim at the farm, I met Rivka Pas-

11. The farm at Czerniaków was originally a halutz (Pioneer Zionist) training kibbutz. It was important during the Ghetto period as a way station for Jewish couriers traveling between cities (see Zuckerman 1993: 75–78 and passim).

12. *Dror*, lit. "freedom": a halutz youth movement in Warsaw led by Antek (Yitzhak Zuckerman).

13. A *sheygets* was a Gentile, usually lower-class, male.

manik, a member of the Zionist Youth, who was two or three years older than me and whom I remembered from the pre-war Zionist Club.[14] Would I go on a mission to the Ghetto? she asked. I agreed at once. The next day, she gave me a small package. I didn't know what was in it, but she told me to put it inside the lining of my coat. (I had to take the lining apart.) I set off for the Ghetto, planning to hide until I could join a group of Jews returning from work. I hid and the Jews came in a line. The German leading them looked away from the group for a moment and I "joined" it in a flash. The Jews suspected I wasn't Jewish, that I had been planted among them as a provocateur. They whispered among themselves about turning me over to the German. I begged them to be-lieve that I was a Jew, and to prove it I started speaking Yid-dish and muttering prayers. Finally, they gave in but warned me I'd have a problem at the gate, since they all had packages of food and I didn't. That problem was solved when one of the Jews gave me part of his food.

Thus I entered the Ghetto. What I saw was a ghost town, whole streets without a living soul, apartments that had been ransacked. I went into some of them out of curiosity: feathers flying in the wind, tatters of clothing were all that was left. I was supposed to go to a certain address and deliver the pack-age to Lutek Rotblatt, then leader of the Zionist Akiba youth movement I belonged to.[15] The meeting with Lutek was emo-

14. Rivka Pasmanik (1921–1943) was born in Czerniaków. She came to Warsaw during the war and was active in Akiba, joining the movement's urban kibbutz at Nalewki 10. She also spent some time at the cooperative farm in Czerniaków. After joining the ZOB, Pas-manik fought in the April Uprising. She committed suicide in the bunker at Mila 18 on May 8, 1943, so as not to be taken alive by the Germans.

15. Lutek Rotblatt (1918–1943), born in Warsaw, was active in Akiba. During the Great Aktsia, he and his mother, Miriam, rescued 80 orphans, whom they hid and supported. Rotblatt worked to ob-

tional, for we hadn't seen each other in several months. We sat and talked until very late, listing the names of members taken in the Great Aktsia, exchanging information about those who were left. In the morning I returned to the farm, minus the package in the lining of my coat.

In early December 1942, the farm in Czerniaków was closed down as a legal workplace and all the Jews there had to move to the Warsaw Ghetto. On the appointed day, the Germans brought all of us into the Ghetto in a caravan. When we were inside the walls, an SS officer comforted us, telling us not to be scared, that everything would be fine.

With the abundance of empty apartments in the Ghetto, my family easily found a flat. I went to work in the warehouses where the Germans collected the property of the Jews who had been cleared out of the Ghetto—gigantic warehouses, full of furniture. Under German supervision, we were driven to the evacuated houses and forced to empty their contents.

By then I belonged to the ZOB and was part of the fighting group at Mila Street 34, where my parents also lived. When the second aktsia began on January 18, 1943, I and my comrades in the ZOB were determined to fight, but we had almost no weapons, except for a few scattered pistols. Our group of a few score members, including Zivia Lubetkin, possessed an arsenal of sticks, knives, iron bars, and anything that came to hand.[16] We holed up in the attic waiting for the Germans

---

tain arms for the ZOB and was appointed commander of the incipient Akiba unit before the April Uprising. He was in the bunker at Mila 18 with his mother; when the situation grew hopeless, he shot her and then killed himself.

Akiba was a small Zionist youth group, part of the halutz movement but not affiliated with any political party.

16. Zivia Lubetkin (1914–1978) was born in Bitan, Polesie (Poland). Active in Dror, she was a central figure in the ZOB, a leader in the January and April Uprisings in the Warsaw Ghetto, and prom-

to come, but they didn't. In other places, where there were weapons, there was shooting, which amazed the Germans. A few of them were killed and their weapons were taken as loot, which apparently was decisive in the struggle. Three days later, the aktsia ceased. The sudden change in their plans resulted from our unforeseen resistance. We couldn't dream of more than that.[17]

Right after the aktsia stopped, I finally succeeded in convincing my parents to leave the Ghetto. I went to make contact with a friend of theirs in a village near Warsaw, Siekierki—a Pole who had offered to help my parents a few months earlier, when they were at the farm in Czerniaków. He had told my mother that if the danger increased and she wanted to hide, he would take her any time. I went to find out if the Pole and his family were still willing to hide my parents: you really had to check everything carefully now. After a long discussion, they agreed to make a hiding place in the hayloft for my parents and sisters. My parents started getting ready; they were especially eager to take their remaining clothes and valuables. In late February or early March, we left the Ghetto for Siekierki. I accompanied my parents there and stayed with them a few hours; then I went back to the Ghetto and to my comrades in the ZOB.

I kept in touch with my parents until the uprising in April 1943. The last time I saw them was late March or early April, a few weeks before the uprising. After that I had no contact with them until the fighters were taken out of the Ghetto on May 10, 1943. I learned that my sister Dina had returned to the Ghetto just before the uprising and had been trapped

---

inent in subsequent resistance activity. The wife of Antek (Yitzhak Zuckerman), she immigrated to Israel in 1946 and was a member of Kibbutz Lohamei Ha-Gettaot.

17. For a more extended account of the January Uprising, see Zuckerman 1993: 263–347.

there; no one knew what had become of her. After inquiring among the fighters, I learned that she had tried to reach me, but the Central Ghetto was cut off from the other parts and she couldn't get to where I was.[18] She was last seen at the end of April, in the area of the Többens-Schultz factory. My parents said she had gone to the Ghetto to bring some distant relatives to the village. Dina was the third oldest of the four children in my family. She was twelve when she was killed.

My parents lived in the hayloft, in a pit prepared for that purpose. You could sit down in it but you couldn't stand upright. I visited them from time to time, but I didn't want to come too often because this was where we had lived before the war and I was known there. Every visit to them was an operation involving a circuitous route, so that I could avoid acquaintances and get into the house without anyone noticing. Of course, every visit was important to my parents and to the landlord as well, since it was one thing to promise something and quite another to keep the promise. My visits had a positive influence on the landlord's attitude toward my parents.

The landlord's son drank a lot and there was some fear that he would leak our secret between drinks. Every time I visited, I spoke harshly to him, indicating to him, with his parents' encouragement, that there was also danger for them. I would hint that I was in the Polish underground and would threaten to wipe him out if he didn't keep the secret.

At a certain point I decided to take my little sister Raya, then ten years old, away from Siekierki. Sitting in the pit for several months wasn't good for her: her legs were wobbly, her face was very pale, and she didn't feel well. In my distress, I appealed to the sisters Anna Wachalska and Marysia Saw-

---

18. The Warsaw Ghetto was divided into three parts: the Central Ghetto, the Brushmakers' Area, and the Többens-Schultz Area.

icka to take Raya into their home.[19] (I'm getting ahead of myself here; I'll tell about the two sisters later.) After I described her situation, the sisters agreed and a few days later I brought her to them. A Jewish girl had been living with Anna, one Zosia Riwak—her real name was Zimra Rawicki—formerly a student at the Dror gymnasium in the Ghetto.[20] She was a bit older than my sister. Both my sister and Zosia looked "good," that is, you couldn't tell them apart from Polish girls. My sister stayed there until Stefan, the hostesses' nephew, was captured by the Gestapo and the two girls had to get out of the apartment at once. My sister was taken to another Polish woman named Janina and later moved with her from Warsaw to nearby Piaseczno.

19. Anna Wachalska and Marysia Sawicka were Polish Christian sisters who provided a great deal of help to the Jews during the war.

20. One of the first underground activities by the halutz youth movements in the Warsaw Ghetto was the establishment of a gymnasium to train future leaders. Subsequently it proved to be a reservoir of members for the resistance movement.

The author,
photographed in
early 1945

The ruins of the Warsaw Ghetto

The author's father's family: from right to left (middle row), brother Israel, mother Miriam, the author, father Zvi holding sister Dina

The author (left) and Tadek Siewierski, with Yitzhak Zuckerman (Antek) in the background

Anna Wachalska

Marysia Sawicka

Leyb (Lutek) Rotblatt

Shlomo (Shlomek) Shuster

Janek Bielak (left) and Yakov Putermilch, photographed by the author in the Wyszków Forest

Warsaw Ghetto fighters in the Wyszków Forest, photographed by the author

2 In the Ranks of the ZOB

The Zionist youth movement I belonged to split and I remained a member of the faction that joined Akiba. Our members were scattered among the various fighting groups; we didn't have an exclusive group of our own, as did Dror, Ha-Shomer Ha-Tza'ir, Gordonia, and other factions in the ZOB.[21] I myself was never really much of a movement person. I was stuck with the name Akiba since everybody in the ZOB took the name of his movement as part of his own, as if it were another last name.

My first contact with the ZOB was my errand to the Ghetto from the farm at Czerniaków in 1942. When I came back to the Ghetto with my parents, I left home and joined the ZOB. After the January Uprising in 1943, I joined Benjamin Wald's group at Leszno Street 60 or 66.[22] The fighting unit was just like a kibbutz: we slept together, ate together, trained together, and performed operations with the same comrades. Among our routine daily operations was keeping watch to avoid unexpected searches by the SS or the Ghetto police. We trained in the use of weapons, emphasizing quick-draw tactics and accuracy of aim. We couldn't do real target shooting, so we aimed at a cardboard target and indicated the points we presumably hit. At one of our quick-draw exercises

21. Dror, Ha-Shomer Ha-Tza'ir, and Gordonia were Zionist-Socialist Pioneer youth movements which advocated immigration to Palestine to build a workers' society and a Jewish state. The 22 fighting units of the ZOB were organized according to movement affiliation.

22. Benjamin Wald (1920–1943) was born in Warsaw and was active in Dror as unit commander in the Többens-Schultz Area. He was killed in early May 1943 at the sewer entrance on Ogrodowa Street, at age 23.

my friend's pistol went off, and it was only thanks to his ineptitude that I wasn't hit.

One day Yitzhak Zuckerman came to visit us at the "base." This was the first time I saw him. I had never been in awe of big shots, and I never imagined that I would soon be working closely with him and that we would go a long way together. Later I heard that he called me "the major link of the ZOB, my aide-de-camp and assistant," but that first meeting in the Ghetto consisted only of the commander's questions and the fighter's answers. At that time Wald and Zuckerman were concerned with the preparation and execution of a death sentence on a collaborator.

Some of the Jews in the Ghetto, who couldn't imagine the evil intentions of the Germans, were steeped in delusions, one of which was that they had to fight the resistance movement and its allies. Other Jews said, "This too shall pass. There have been similar things in the history of our nation." Religious people put their faith in God. Some in the Ghetto were simple cowards, paralyzed with fear. Others were collaborators. "Purges," even though inevitable, were the hardest thing for us. I don't intend to go into this subject. No doubt Yitzhak Zuckerman had to make such painful and difficult decisions.[23]

One of the organization's first operations in which I participated was the release of Jewish prisoners held by the Jewish police in the Ghetto jail. The prisoners were slated to be turned over to the Gestapo a day or two later, and the Jewish Fighting Organization decided to free them—at any cost. If memory serves, the prisoners included some members of the ZOB who had been denounced as belonging to the underground organization. The Germans used the Jewish police and made tremendous efforts to track them down. It was important to the ZOB to free this group. I was to reconnoiter the jail and

23. See Zuckerman 1993: 324–325.

gather information about the people inside, the location of the cells, and other vital details. I gained entry on the pretext that one of my relatives was imprisoned there and I wanted to give him a package of food. First, however, I asked what could be included in a package—just food or also clothes?—and other questions. It was dusk, I went in, asked my questions, talked with the police on duty, looked around, and photographed the situation in my memory as best I could.

The information I brought served as the basis for our extremely simple plan. Several members of the organization were assigned to enter the jail the next day at dusk. We were to overpower the police, open the cells, free the prisoners, and leave. I was to be the first one in, to divert the guards' attention for a few seconds and say I had brought a package for one of the prisoners. Then my accomplices would come in immediately, indicate that we were members of the ZOB, threaten the police with guns, and carry out the operation. That's just what we did. At the designated time, I went in and started talking with the police; right behind me, several ZOB members burst in, wearing masks, with guns drawn. We made all the police lie down on the floor next to one another. Some of us opened or, more precisely, burst open the cell doors and yelled at the prisoners, "We are freeing you." We urged them to get away and go into hiding. Everything went smoothly.

This operation, one of the first bold acts of the ZOB, impressed the Jews in the Ghetto and scared the Jewish police. It was decisive in the struggle for control of the Ghetto between the Judenrat and the ZOB. We became famous. Reports spread like wildfire and came back to us with a personal touch: apparently the operation had been commanded by one of the fighters from the Polish underground—me. (I wasn't wearing a mask and the Jews thought I was a Gentile.) In any event, the operation had an impact and the population began to believe in the ZOB, whereas the Jewish police of the Judenrat were humiliated and their image tarnished in the eyes of the population.

Our major occupation was acquiring weapons, which naturally were very expensive. Since we had absolutely no sources of funding, we had to get money from rich Jews and did a lot of detective work about their financial situation and living conditions, the possibilities of getting in and out, and so on. These operations took place at night. We would get into an apartment and try to convince the person to give us the money we needed, without using force. Once we burst into an apartment where one of the tenants previously had given us all the necessary details and even opened the door to us. (Of course, we pretended we didn't know him, and to complete the deception, the man even started a squabble with us.) Diamonds were hidden in the lamps and we naturally requisitioned them.

Some time after that operation, I was transferred to another fighting group, in the Brushmakers' Area, commanded by Hanoch Gutman, whose base was at Swietojerska Street 32 or 43.[24] I don't know why I was transferred from Wald's group to Gutman's. I was simply told that I was to go to another group, and I had no reason not to obey the order. I moved to the Brushmakers' Area and stayed with Gutman's group up to the time of the uprising, until I was sent to the Aryan side to make contact with Antek.

Shimek Becomes Kazik

The Ghetto wasn't very big anymore, but each area was separate and the character of a fighting group was largely deter-

24. Hanoch Gutman, born in Lodz, was active in Dror and the ZOB. He fought in the January and April Uprisings, served as commander in the Többens-Schultz Area until March 1943 and later in the Brushmakers' Area, and was wounded on May 2, 1943. The circumstances of his death at age 22 are unknown.

mined by its commander. Each one had a different approach, style, and method of issuing orders. Gutman was brief and sharp in military matters, but with friends he was courteous and understanding. By this time—February or March 1943—we members of ZOB were convinced that we had to act, that sitting around idly was to risk our lives. Our environment wasn't very encouraging. The relatively few Jews left in the Ghetto were generally not enthusiastic about our operations. Thus the ZOB was in a double underground, hiding from the Germans and from most of the Jews as well. We got sympathy and good will only from a small group who were close to us.

The relationships formed within the groups—the attachments and friendships between the fighters—were very important. We were all young and belonged to a halutz Zionist youth movement. Dvora Baran, a member of my group, belonged to Dror.[25] Dvora and I were close. I had met her at the farm in Czerniaków, where she lived with a Dror group. She wasn't from Warsaw and our lives had been different: she came from Wolyn province (in eastern Poland), attended a Hebrew Tarbut school and was in the He-Halutz Ha-Tza'ir youth movement (which united with Frayhayt to form Dror).[26] She dreamed of forests and the fragrance of flowers.

25. Dvora Baran was born in Kowel, joined He-Halutz Ha-Tza'ir, and moved to Warsaw during the war. She fought in the April Uprising in the Brushmakers' Area. When the unit's bunker on Franciszkanska Street was surrounded on May 2, 1943, the commander assigned her to go first and find a way of escape for the dozens of fighters still in the bunker. Surprising the Germans with her beauty and boldness, she caught them off guard and hurled a grenade into their ranks, thus allowing the fighters to leave the shelter and engage in a battle in which four Jews and dozens of Germans were killed. The Germans returned the next day and she was killed in the fighting at age 23.

26. Tarbut schools were Hebrew secular schools established in eastern Europe, especially Poland, between the wars. Frayhayt was

When the Ghetto was burning and the smell of scorched objects and bodies filled our noses, she said she missed the odor of the forests in Wolyn. Before the war, she had trained at Kibbutz Borokhov in Lodz, where she had worked in the sewing workshop. When she was transferred to Warsaw, she got involved in educational activities. She was very pretty and charming, and devoted to the movement and its values. You might say she was cut to the measure of the movement; in other words, she and the movement were one and the same.

My transfer from Wald's group to Hanoch Gutman's might have had something to do with Dvora; as a member of Dror, she belonged to Hanoch's group, and since I had to move, I chose to be with her.

Our acquaintance in the fighting group turned into young love. To carry on an affair at that time in the Brushmakers' Area was really something! Our commander, Hanoch, had a girlfriend. As far as we were concerned, they were married, even though they hadn't had a proper ceremony. When Hanoch was wounded in battle, in the April Uprising, his girlfriend didn't want to leave and stayed to take care of him. As for me and Dvora, the group sensed that something was shaping up between us. Relations in the group of men and women were kind and understanding. Anyway, it was hard to tell who were "couples": the leaders of the halutz movement were loyal to "sexual purity," and affairs were mostly platonic. Couples talked a lot, exchanged feelings, dreamed.

Dvora and I grew closer. When Hanoch found out, he called us in and scolded us for keeping our relationship secret. If he had known, he said, he would have celebrated. When the uprising erupted, we wound up in the bunker at Franciszkanska Street 22. I wanted very much to be with Dvora. We lay huddled together on the floor of the bunker.

a Zionist-Socialist youth movement. The more Yiddish-oriented Frayhayt joined He-Halutz Ha-Tza'ir in 1939 to form Dror.

Above us, on bunk beds along the wall, were more people. We lay very close to each another and agreed not to restrain ourselves; she asked me if I had a prophylactic and of course I didn't—so we lay and talked all night.

After I left the Ghetto on behalf of the ZOB command, Dvora was killed along with many other members of the group. The Germans had discovered and surrounded the bunker. Our companions said that during the battle for the bunker Dvora had found the strength to spur the fighters on. One of those killed was my good friend Abraham Eiger.[27] As he lay wounded, he insulted and cursed the Germans and challenged them to approach him. They didn't dare and came close only after pumping a full magazine of ammunition into his body, which they then mutilated.

I was told that, in the bunker, Dvora was heard saying something like: "We've got a whole night ahead of us, life is safe until dawn, after three days of fighting; I don't know if those of us who survive will be able to appreciate that in days to come. We can expect hard battles and every day that passes when they don't break us is unbelievable. I still believe we can get even, even after a week of war. Meanwhile, who knows, maybe help will come from somewhere. Hold fast."

At Hanoch's order, we went on "exes" (short for expropriations) to "raise" money from rich Jews. We kept watch at the home of one man, collected information, and set a date for the operation. The apartment was on the second floor. One of us knocked on the door and when it opened we burst in, identified the man of the house, stood facing him in a "persuasive" movement, and announced, "We've come to get your contribution for the ZOB." The Jew refused. I put the barrel of my revolver near him; he froze and didn't utter a

27. Abraham Eiger was a member of Dror and the ZOB who came to Warsaw in 1942. He participated in the April Uprising in the Brushmakers' Area and died fighting at age 20.

sound. Then Hanoch ordered, "Kazik, kill him!" When he called me "Kazik," I was to understand that I had to appear as Kazik, that is, as a Pole. I assumed a strange expression, rolled my eyes, puffed up my chest, grabbed the Jew by the collar, and dragged him into a corner of the room. "Listen, with me you don't play games!" I told him. When he heard the name "Kazik," he understood he was dealing with a Gentile, and you didn't get smart with a Gentile, especially not in those days. He broke down, asked for a brief delay, went to a hiding place, pulled out some money, and reluctantly gave us his "contribution."

Ever since then, the name Kazik has stuck to me.

These actions weren't exactly my pride and joy. Naturally, I preferred to work against the Germans, but circumstances dictated our methods. Without money, we couldn't prepare for the uprising, acquire weapons, support the fighters. "Taking care of" those who denounced and turned Jews in was not to my liking either. But did we have a choice?

The "sniffers"—our intelligence people—identified a very rich Jew in the Brushmakers' Area. We considered how to get money out of him after he refused to contribute willingly. At headquarters it was decided to take his beautiful daughter hostage. One day I led a band of three to the man's house. On some pretext or other, we asked his daughter to accompany us. I walked next to her, while my two companions followed at a short distance. As we walked, she sensed that something was wrong. She stared, suspecting that the story we had told wasn't quite straight and that we had other intentions. She wanted to go back home. It was about eleven o'clock in the morning. The street was teeming with people and we were afraid of running into a German patrol. I was forced to reveal who I was and to explain to her that there was no way back: she *had* to go with us or else we would have to use force. I hinted that we were armed and that if she tried to run away, it was liable to "end up badly." Smiling meaningfully, I added, "We're not interested in that." The girl understood the situation and went on walking with us.

I was wearing the sort of leather coat adopted by those who collaborated with the Gestapo, and it attracted attention. Even though the distance from the Jew's house to the ZOB "jailhouse" was only a few hundred meters, there was great danger. Passers-by were beginning to look at us suspiciously—a young man in a leather coat holding a girl by the arm and dragging her along behind him. My companions were tense, their weapons ready for action. We took the girl to a locked room in an attic in the Brushmakers' Area. We explained that we had nothing against her and that our only object was to force her father to contribute money to the organization. If he responded, we would release her immediately. The girl was asked to write a letter to her father, which we dictated to her and delivered to her house by messenger. The girl was pretty and I was sorry to meet her in such circumstances, but I had to do my job. Once again I played a Christian, a representative of the Polish underground, supposedly cooperating with the ZOB in the Ghetto.

Soon after, the father was brought to the jailhouse. He was very worried about his daughter's safety and had decided to come on his own to prove to himself that nothing bad had happened to her. After the man was brought into the locked room, the three of us had to try to squeeze out of him a sum of money which, according to our information, he was capable of paying. He was a real character. Despite our threats of execution, he claimed he couldn't give such a large sum. In fact, at first he demanded that we release him and his daughter for nothing. This went on for two or three days, while father and daughter were held prisoner. A few times a day we'd try again, threaten, but he stood firm.

As a last resort, my commanders decided to include me in an attempt to "convince" him, so he would know he wasn't dealing with "compassionate Jews" but with real Gentiles, for whom killing a man, not to mention a Jew, was not a problem to hesitate about. When I appeared in the prison room, we started talking politely. I brought up our demands again. But he stood his ground. We had agreed from the start that, at a certain stage, we'd begin to play the role of "murderer," that is, we'd put him up against the wall, cock our weapons, count to three, according to all the rules of executions, hoping the man would finally break. Hence, when I didn't succeed in convincing him with the carrot, I was forced to use the stick of execution. I followed the script. The man was stood in the corner. I cocked the weapon in my hand. My finger was on the trigger. I said, "I'll shoot you if you don't respond." The man broke down and for the first time started negotiating the amount. I wasn't sure if my threats had influenced him. Perhaps he hadn't broken at all but was only pretending because he wanted me to save his daughter. The man believed a Gentile was standing in front of him, a pure Aryan. Apparently, I impressed him as a man to be trusted. After he agreed to "contribute," he started persuading me to agree to take his daughter to the Aryan side and hide her there. I was forced to continue the game since I couldn't tell him I wasn't a Pole. I promised him I'd think about it and, if I did agree, I'd come to his apartment in a few days and we'd discuss the details.

We devoted a lot of energy to preparing for our engagement with the Germans. We dug tunnels under the road—for a few dozen meters—from the gate of the Ghetto, which the Germans used whenever they came to carry out the aktsias, and to the Brushmakers' Area. We thought the date of the liquidation of the Ghetto was approaching. It was tremendously hard work to dig the tunnel, especially because we had to keep it secret even from the Ghetto residents themselves. When we finished, we prepared a surprise for the Germans: a big load of explosives, placed in the tunnel under the gate, ready to be set off from a distance at the right moment.

Once we received information, which turned out to be false, that there was a supply of fuel in a certain place not far from the Ghetto. We went out and dug, but we didn't find anything and returned empty-handed.

We lived in crowded conditions. We shared our little bit of food. During our free time we would sit and talk and dream of better days. Sometimes I'd bring up crazy ideas about going out and beating up Germans. The group understood my mood but, by nature, they were disciplined and trained to be part of a group. Acting together was in their blood.

In the days before the decisive aktsia, on April 19, 1943, we sat in our apartment base and sang "songs of the homeland."[28]

In Battle, under the Command of Hanoch Gutman

We knew the day we would start shooting wasn't far off. When my turn came to stand guard, I would sit at the observation post, as required by ZOB discipline, and various thoughts would go through my mind: Wouldn't it be better to go out and attack the Germans, to shoot and kill them? The observation post was connected to the base by an alarm bell. I was on edge, impatient; something urged me to "pull the trigger." I played with the gun I had just gotten—a WIS, a Polish revolver. I rolled a grenade or a Molotov cocktail in my hand. In training, especially in quick draw and escape, I was good; but I was fed up with pointless exercises.

From where I stood, I could see the street. It was different than it had been a month before, and certainly than it had been a year earlier. Before the war I wasn't familiar with that area. I had almost never been in a crowded Jewish quarter. I felt stifled and as if my hands were tied; the observation post was cramped. Hanoch Gutman's group at Walowa Street 6

---

28. I.e., Zionist songs from Eretz Israel.

(the corner of Swietojerska Street 34) numbered ten fighters, including four girls. As in the other fighting groups in the Brushmakers' Area, there was a sense of expectation; we hadn't yet opened fire on the enemy.

We had heard the couriers' reports about the clashes with Germans and the other events of the previous day in the Central Ghetto. With their own eyes they had seen Germans killed. The news excited me even more: I wanted to get into the action! It wasn't long before it came: the Brushmakers' Area was surrounded by gendarmes and Ukrainian mercenaries. I stood on a balcony facing Walowa Street. Germans and Ukrainians were visible beyond the wall. From time to time they shot at our windows, just for fun, while we had orders to hold our fire.

On April 19, at four in the morning, we saw German soldiers crossing the Nalewki intersection on their way to the Central Ghetto, walking in an endless procession. Behind them were tanks, armored vehicles, light cannons, and hundreds of Waffen-SS units on motorcycles.[29] "They look like they're going to war," I said to Zippora, my companion at the post. Suddenly I felt how very weak we were. What force did we have against an army, against tanks and armored vehicles? We had nothing but pistols and grenades. I didn't get depressed. Finally, the time came to settle accounts with them. Sounds of rifle and machine gun fire and grenade explosions reached us from the Central Ghetto. We distinguished between one shot and another: "That's a German, that's ours," we would determine. "Here, that's our mine, our grenade." Calm prevailed for a day in our area. At dusk came a letter from the Többens-Schultz factory calling on everyone to come to work, "since there won't be any aktsia in the Brushmakers' Area." At dusk we left our positions, left scouts in the observation post, and went to the unit base. We

29. The Waffen-SS were SS combat units.

had been in a state of readiness for several days, but now we made high-level preparations: everyone held the weapons and supplies he had been issued.

As I said, we had planted a large quantity of explosives near the Brushmakers' gate, under the street. One day after the Germans began liquidating the Ghetto—on April 20—as I stood at the observation post near the gate, I suddenly saw an SS unit approaching. With one hand I pushed the alarm button, and with the other I grabbed the fuse to the explosives. At that moment my commander, Hanoch, burst in, snatched the fuse out of my hand, and, after waiting a few seconds, exploded the mine. I was nailed to the spot, almost paralyzed—a tremendous explosion! I had a fervent desire to see it with my own eyes. And I did see: crushed bodies of soldiers, limbs flying, cobblestones and fences crumbling, complete chaos. I saw and I didn't believe: German soldiers screaming in panicky flight, leaving their wounded behind. I pulled out one grenade and then another and tossed them. My comrades were also shooting and firing at them. We weren't marksmen but we did hit some. The Germans took off. But they came back later, fearful, their fingers on their triggers. They didn't walk, they ran next to the walls. We let the first group of six pass—a shame to waste ammunition on a small group. Then we burst out, with two homemade grenades, ten Molotov cocktails, and pistols in our hands. "Shlomek—the gasoline!" I shouted to one of my comrades, and hurled a grenade at the Germans. We threw the Molotov cocktails at them and they burst into flames, so we shot at the fire. A waste of the only grenade we had, and we retreated up the street, taking a position with the rest of the fighters. Quiet prevailed.

The Germans ran away, but they came back half an hour later. We welcomed them with Molotov cocktails and grenades. One of the Germans, seeing a girl at the post, called out in amazement: "Hans, look! A woman!" and started shooting at her. But she didn't retreat. Protecting themselves with a strong fire cover, the Germans began withdrawing. One of our fighters, who had taken a position in the attic, poured shots onto the Germans near the walls, in spite of the heavy fire coming from there, and killed six of them. In the yard of a large building fronting on Swietojerska and Walowa streets, Dr. Laus, one of the leaders of the Brushmakers' Area, appeared with two Germans in uniform. They were waving rifles as a sign that their intentions were peaceful. As they went from house to house, Dr. Laus called on the Fighting Organization to put down its weapons within fifteen minutes. We replied with shooting. One of the Germans was killed. Dr. Laus ran away.

Some time later, the Germans returned carrying stretchers and gathered up their wounded. We took advantage of the lull to leap to another position. The enemy began using automatic weapons, machine guns and flame throwers. They avoided coming into the Ghetto in orderly files and adopted the tactics of fighting in a populated area. Now the real siege began: the sounds of all kinds of weapons blended together—cannons, machine guns, mortars, light weapons. We all held our positions and the enemy was invisible. Despair! There was nobody to fight! The Germans took positions outside the wall and poured hellfire onto us. Suddenly, flames surrounded the building: flames and stifling smoke forced us to leave our positions. Three men covered our retreat; when we found there was nothing more we could do in the Brushmakers' Area, we decided to withdraw.

There was no advance plan for withdrawal, and not knowing what direction to turn made our situation difficult. In the chaos, I went to scout out a retreat route. I took this job because I looked Aryan, and I was wearing an SS uniform that allowed me to move around in the daytime. But there was a danger that fighters in other groups, seeing me from a distance, would think I really was an SS man and would open fire on me. As I searched, I came on a bunker at Swietojerska Street 34. When I started down, the people in the bunker saw first my boots and then my SS coat, and started screaming. I had trouble calming them down in time. We didn't think the bunker was a fit place for our group and we continued searching until we found another, well-built bunker, completely underground, whose inhabitants agreed to take us. After we gathered the whole group in that bunker, we started looking for the other two groups of the organization, with whom we had lost contact. We wanted to turn this bunker into a gathering point for all the fighting groups in the Brushmakers' Area. Gradually, the groups began to assemble.

As commander of the mission, I had to appoint people to scout. This wasn't hard, since they volunteered. We went to search for our comrades. On the way, we came on some Germans but didn't get into battle with them. A few times we tried in vain to make contact with the other groups. As we retreated, Marek Edelman, Hanoch Gutman, and I went to scout the way to the new position on Franciszkanska Street.[30] I saw houses burning. Panicky Jews ran out, straight into the German line of fire. I tried to ignore what I saw. I clung to my mission—to find a safe and quick way to rescue my companions. Then we came on the body of Michal Klepfisz.[31]

30. Marek Edelman, born in Warsaw, was active in the Bund from his youth. (The Bund, or General Jewish Workers' Union, was a social-democratic party that advocated a Yiddish secular culture in the Diaspora.) He was a member of the ZOB command staff and commander of the Brushmakers' Area in the April Uprising. He escaped through the sewers to Aryan Warsaw and fought in the Polish Uprising. Edelman is currently a cardiologist in Lodz.

31. Michal Klepfisz (1913–1943), born in Warsaw, was an active Bundist and a member of the ZOB. On the Aryan side he assisted Arye Wilner (ZOB liaison with the Polish underground) and obtained weapons and the formula for Molotov cocktails. He fought in the April Uprising and was killed in a clash with the Germans at age 30.

Michal was an engineer, our "operations man"; with the help of comrades, he had set up a small "factory" to make Molotov cocktails. It was he who had made and planted the mine that had exploded a short while before. We didn't find his revolver on him; the Germans had certainly taken it. Before then, after the first battle, my friend Shlomo Shuster and I noticed two Jews trying to get out of the Ghetto.[32] When we stopped them, we found documents proving that they were Gestapo agents. We took the documents from them and sent them off, figuring that the Germans would destroy them and that it would be too bad to waste our few bullets on them.

Finally, we met our two groups, who were also looking for us. We gathered all of them, eighty to a hundred members of the ZOB, in the bunker at Swietojerska 34. The people of the bunker welcomed us warmly. These "ordinary Jews" wanted to join our ranks, but unfortunately we didn't have enough weapons. The echoes of explosions and the constant rumble of machine gun fire reached us. All night long we were busy cleaning our weapons, checking the bullets and the grenade fuses. Finally, we imposed a short rest on ourselves. In the evening, a few comrades went out to bring back Michal's body and to dig a grave for him in one of the courtyards. We dug in silence. Night fell and, between isolated shots, a momentary silence descended on the Ghetto.

To the Central Ghetto

All day long patrols of the Jewish Fighting Organization covered the Brushmakers' Area, but the Germans kept out of

32. Shlomo Shuster (1926–1943) was born in Pruszków and moved to Warsaw with his family in 1941. He joined a Dror fighting unit and was one of the bravest fighters in the Brushmakers' Area during the April Uprising. He escaped through the sewers to Aryan Warsaw on May 8, 1943, but was killed when he returned to the Ghetto on a rescue mission.

sight. At dusk, people whose bunkers had been burned down began streaming to us; many had been burned alive. The area was engulfed in flames. The organization hadn't prepared bunkers, since that ran counter to its purpose; and those that were prepared had been built by private initiative. Some were well built, others were hastily thrown together at the last minute. With the fire rampaging through every house in the Ghetto, the situation in the bunkers became untenable. Our bunker was filled with smoke, and when we were forced to leave it, we decided to make our way to the Central Ghetto. We assembled in the courtyard before we left, standing in straight rows. I shall never forget the picture of the gathering: it was night, but the flames made it bright as day. Everything all around was on fire, walls were crashing down. We had to go through burning shops, with flames surrounding us on all sides. The heat was unbearable. Slivers of glass in the yards were melted.

We put wet cloths on our faces. Our goal was to get to Franciszkanska Street 20. We only had to cross the street. Nothing seems easier, but the wall along Bonifraterska Street at the intersection, as well as the wall separating the Brush-makers' Area from no-man's-land, had been destroyed. We were exposed to the patrols of Latvians, Ukrainians, and Germans lying in wait for us at the breaches in the wall. It was possible to reach the Central Ghetto only through one gap. Despite the danger, we succeeded and only one group, with which we lost contact, failed. Shlomo Shuster and I served as guides. The members jumped through the gap after they got a signal from us.

We knew that a German tank had been set on fire in the Central Ghetto and that dozens of Germans had been killed in the uprising.[33] Our losses were few. In the first three days

33. According to Gen. Jürgen Stroop, the commander of the German forces that suppressed the uprising, the casualty rate among

the Germans didn't take a single Jew out of the buildings. After their attempts to penetrate the Ghetto had failed, they decided to to spare themselves casualties by destroying it from outside with cannon and aerial bombings. A few days later the Ghetto was totally destroyed. Those who survived continued living in bunkers. Apparently the Germans concluded there weren't many Jews left in the Ghetto and decided it was safe to enter during the day. At night they were careful and stayed outside: control of the Ghetto was in the hands of the ZOB, and we could walk around among the ruins without fear. So all communications operations between the groups, provisioning, and searching for survivors or bodies took place at night.

I was in charge of reconnaissance, visited all the positions, and had a chance to meet all the members of the organization who were there. In the Central Ghetto, we gathered in the "Gepner" bunker, underneath the central food supply warehouses at Franciszkanska 22.[34] When we got there, the bunker—a big cellar—was already overfull. The stifling heat was unbearable; people behaved like complete lunatics, ready to steal food from one another at gunpoint. We weren't surprised by the almost friendly reception we received, because when only a handful of Jews were left in the Ghetto, everyone finally understood—unfortunately too late—that the fighters weren't the "enemies of the people."

We went out to search for food in empty bunkers and cellars. Once we went down to a cellar whose walls emitted

---

the Nazis was more modest. He claims 16 killed and 85 wounded (Stroop 1979).

34. Abraham Gepner (1872–1943) was head of the Supply Department in the Judenrat. He was sympathetic to the ZOB and especially to the halutz underground. In early 1942 he helped the ZOB a great deal. He was killed in the April Uprising, after the battles of May 3 in the Franciszkanska Street bunker.

waves of heat. My companions and I found ourselves walking on a kind of soft, light ground, like feathers. It was ash with scorched bodies lying in it. In a corner we came on a barrel of honey. We dipped our hands in it and it was almost boiling. We licked that honey until we got sick. At night we continued our reconnaissance patrols. The "streets" were nothing but rows of smoldering ruins. It was hard to cross them without stepping on charred bodies. Once I came on a heap of bodies and heard a child's weeping. As I approached, I saw a woman's dead body hugging a living infant. I stood still a moment and then went on walking.

One night, before dawn on a Friday, a reconnaissance patrol went out to contact fighting groups in the Central Ghetto. Two men went toward Gesia Street, Jurek and I turned toward Nalewki. The street was full of corpses, and to avoid trampling on them we had to leap from place to place. At Nalewki 36 we came on a group of fighters commanded by Lutek. From that moment, constant contact was renewed with the command of the Fighting Organization and all the groups. At that time no planned activities were being carried out except for skirmishes with patrols. Three days later we were forced to leave that bunker, which had served as a base for our sorties. We moved to no-man's-land but had to leave there too because of the flames and the stifling smoke. The situation in the bunkers was depressing, hopeless—no air, no water, and no food. One day passed and another, and on the tenth day of the aktsia the Ghetto was burned down.

In this dreadful situation, unable to continue the war for lack of weapons, unable to engage the enemy in battle since they no longer came into the Ghetto, we had the idea of getting our people out to the city in order to continue fighting there. On April 29 the command staff—Mordechai Anielewicz, Zivia Lubetkin, Michael Rosenfeld, and Hirsh Berlinski—met to discuss the situation.[35] We had no delusions about the future of the burning Ghetto. They decided to send messengers to the Aryan side, to the representative of the Fighting Organization, Antek, who had been there for two weeks.[36]

After eleven or twelve days of battle, most of the fighters were still alive. The Germans continued destroying the Ghetto from outside, with artillery bombardments and air attacks; finally, sappers were sent to set fires and explode every cellar and bunker. In this situation, we couldn't get into a battle with them anyway, and it was only a question of time until we would all be buried alive under the debris. The command staff therefore decided to find a way to rescue the fighters who could still be saved so they could continue fighting

35. Mordechai Anielewicz (1919–1943), born in Warsaw, was active in the leadership of Ha-Shomer Ha-Tza'ir, as an editor of the underground press, and as an educator. He was close to the organizers of the Ringelblum Archives, who collected historical documentation of the Warsaw Ghetto. Appointed ZOB commander in September 1942, he led the April Uprising and was killed with his companions in the bunker at Mila 18 on May 8, 1943.

Michael Rosenfeld, a graduate of Warsaw University, was active in the PPR (Polska Partia Robotnicza, or Polish Workers' party, i.e., the Communists) and a member of the ZOB command staff. He fought in the Central Ghetto in April 1943 and escaped through the sewers. He was killed in a clash with the Germans when he was about 30.

Hirsh Berlinski (1908–1944), born in Lodz, was active in the armed resistance movement and represented Po'alei Zion Left on the ZOB command staff. He fought in the April Uprising and escaped through the sewers to the Aryan side. He was killed in the Polish Uprising.

36. Antek had been sent to the Aryan side by the ZOB command staff on April 13, 1943, to act as liaison with the Polish.

the Germans under other conditions. At first an experiment was made: a small group would make contact with Antek and get advice about smuggling the rest of the fighters out of the Ghetto. But the attempt to send emissaries failed and several members were killed. Tuvia Borzykowski was in one of these groups.[37] He was lucky and survived after his group was attacked by a German patrol. Hella Schüpper was in the second group.[38] Other attempts also failed, but I can't remember who took part in them.

37. Tuvia Borzykowski, born in Lodz, was active in Dror and the ZOB in the January and April Uprisings. He escaped to the Aryan side and fought in the Polish Uprising. In 1949 he immigrated to Israel, where he died ten years later, aged 48.

38. Hella Rufeisen-Schüpper was born in Krakow and attended a Polish Catholic school, which came in handy for her later underground work. A member of Akiba and of the ZOB in Warsaw, she was sent to Krakow in August 1942, where she served as a ZOB courier, smuggling weapons, people, and information. After the uprising in Krakow in December 1942, she was arrested by the Germans while trying to enter the Warsaw Ghetto. She escaped but was wounded and remained in the Ghetto until the April Uprising. On May 8, 1943, she was sent to the Aryan side to contact Antek. In the summer of 1943 she was caught in the trap of Hotel Polski (see Shulman 1982) and was shipped to Bergen-Belsen concentration camp, where she survived until the liberation in April 1945. She now lives in Israel.

3 To the Sewers: Rescue of the Remnant

Mission to the Aryan Side

Despite these failures, the command staff decided to send Zygmunt Fryderych, a Bundist, and me to make another attempt to contact our companions on the Aryan side.[39] We used the tunnel dug by the Jewish Military Union (the Revisionists), which we had discovered on one of our expeditions to seek a way out of the Ghetto.[40] Before the uprising the local commanders of the two organizations had made contact to coordinate future operations. During the uprising we heard that there had been a fierce battle between the Revisionist Military Union and the Germans and that the Jewish fighters had decided to cross to the Aryan side in coordination with the Polish underground (a faction of the AK).[41] Later we learned that they had fled through that tunnel

39. Zygmunt Fryderych (1911–1943) was born in Warsaw, served as liaison in Aryan Warsaw, and smuggled arms into the Ghetto. He returned to the Ghetto and participated in the April Uprising. In May 1943, on the Aryan side, he was killed by Polish police while leading a group of fighters to shelter. See Meed (1979: 157–158) for details of his death.

40. The Jewish Military Union, or ZZW (Zydowskie Zwiazek Wojskowy), was the organization of right-wing Zionists who refused to join the ZOB and formed an independent army in the Ghetto. Gutman (1989: 348) estimates their fighting force at the time of the April Uprising at 200–250. Their main force was destroyed in a battle with the Germans on the second or third day of the uprising; most of the survivors escaped to the Aryan side through a tunnel they had dug and were killed in attacks by German troops and Polish police. See Gutman 1989: 376–377 for details.

41. The AK (Armia Krajowa), or Home Army, was generally right-

under Bonifraterska Street. The Ghetto wall divided the street in the middle: the odd numbers were inside the Ghetto and the even numbers were on the Aryan side.

We assembled a few items we might need on the Aryan side, things like a shirt and sweater. We had no identity papers. Hochberg and Lolek accompanied us to the entrance.[42] We said good-bye, descended into the tunnel—and there we were on the Aryan side. We hid in an attic until morning because we had to familiarize ourselves with the area. Moreover, it was better not to walk around outside after curfew. At dawn we went downstairs and peeked outside. Clear signs of battle remained in the courtyard. All of a sudden we were surprised by a Christian Pole who appeared in one of the doorways. I immediately began a story I made up on the spot: the two of us had gotten stuck with the Jews in the Ghetto; we had gone in to deal in clothes and were caught in the uprising; only now had we somehow managed to get out. The man was convinced, congratulated us on escaping from the Ghetto, and even told us how to get out of the building without running into the nearby German patrol, whose function, he said, was to guard the Ghetto from outside. He also told us that a group of armed Jews from the Ghetto had been holed up in his house not long before. They had been caught in the building by the Gestapo and the SS, and there had been a fight, whose "results you can still see," he said, pointing to the yard and the rooms. Indeed, we did see bodies on the roof, bullet cases, holes in the walls—confirmation of the event. According to him, a few

wing, with some anti-Semitic factions. It took its orders from the Polish Government-in-Exile in London.

42. Adolf Hochberg, born in Germany, was a member of Dror who fought in the Brushmakers' Area. One of those who left the Ghetto through the sewers, he died at age 21 while trying to round up the other fighters.

of the group had made off in a car apparently provided by "outsiders."

Later I learned that these were indeed members of the Revisionist group, who had used the tunnel when they decided to leave the Ghetto and go to the Aryan side. Zygmunt and I followed the man's instructions and avoided the gap in one of the walls. We were on our way to Krzyzanowski Street 44, to the apartment of Anna Wachalska and her sister, Marysia Sawicka. We hadn't gone far when we were joined by a group of blackmailers who had immediately recognized that we were Jews and who tried to extort whatever we had. We didn't have anything valuable and I realized that unless we got rid of them, they would turn us over to the Germans. I glanced around and thought quickly. As I looked, a truck passing by in the street came into my field of vision. At once we ran and climbed on from behind. By the time the blackmailers understood what was going on, we were far away. The truck picked up speed as we hung on. At the corner it slowed down, and we jumped off unhurt and moved on to our destination.

Walking swiftly and strenuously—we were weak after several days without food—we reached Anna's house and rang the doorbell. Anna, the widow of a PPS (Polska Partia Socjalistyczna, or Polish Socialist party) activist, knew Zygmunt well and greeted us warmly. Zygmunt introduced me and we were joined by Marysia Sawicka. The women suggested we wash and change our clothes. This was my first shower since April 18, an opportunity not only to wash my body but also to restore my soul. When I went into the bright bathroom, covered with white tiles, and was given soap and a fragrant towel—it was like a dream. It was hard for me to believe that, just a few hours before, I had been in another world, between the crumbling walls of the Ghetto, where everything beyond the walls seemed inaccessible. We shaved and washed and put on the clothes we were given, which belonged to a relative, Stefan Szewerski. We were invited to the dining room, to a table covered with a white cloth, loaded with food: an abundance of bread, sausages, and even vodka.

The welcome of the two women whom I had just met dazzled me, but I didn't forget why we had come. That very day, or perhaps the next, their cousin Stefan sent us to Feigl Peltel, who lived under the assumed name of Wladka at Barakowa Street 2.[43] Wladka was the courier of the Bund on the Aryan side of Warsaw. Her apartment became a base of operations to rescue the fighters left behind in the Ghetto. We wanted to get in touch immediately with Antek, the ZOB representative on the Aryan side. He showed up that afternoon with Franya Beatus, his courier, and Tadek (Tuvia Shayngut).[44] We reported on the situation in the Ghetto, speaking in disjointed fragments, piling details on top of one another. We named every person who had been killed. We described the deployment of the fighting groups, told of the systematic destruction and the hopelessness of the situation. (Later I learned that after she heard our report, Franya Beatus committed suicide. She had done her job loyally and effectively. Antek didn't talk much about her afterward, but when he did, it was with great praise.)[45]

Our discussion focused on how to save our comrades. In

43. Wladka Meed, who currently lives in New York.

44. Tuvia Shayngut (Szejngut) served as liaison with the AL (Armia Ludowa, or People's Army, the leftist Polish underground army) on the Aryan side. Wladka Meed describes him as "a sturdy, towheaded young lad [who] wore heavy high boots and a farmer's long overcoat and had the looks and ways of a peasant. . . . He was both shrewd and fearless, undeterred by obstacles. He always carried a revolver, and declared that he would never be captured alive" (1979: 97).

45. Franya Beatus came to Warsaw from Ostrowiec in late 1942 and served as a courier for the ZOB. She was about 17 when she died. For a more extended account of her death, see Zuckerman 1993: 385.

my naiveté I had thought ways could be found immediately. But it soon became apparent that "nobody was standing and waiting for us on the Aryan side" and that if we wanted to rescue anybody, we would have to do it ourselves. That was the message I absorbed clearly. We agreed that, given the circumstances, each of us—using his or her contacts—would try to do something to rescue the fighters in the Ghetto. We learned that, aside from those present, we could get help from Stefan Szewerski, our hostesses, Kostek, and Stefan Pokropek. We agreed on methods of communication and set another meeting in the near future. We already understood that our essential problems were: how to get back into the Ghetto; how to bring the fighters out; where to house and hide them afterward; and how to transport them.

The solution was to make contact with the sewer workers, who knew their way around that labyrinthine, complex system and could lead us back to the Ghetto on a route we could also use to remove those who had survived. At this point all of us—using our connections on the Aryan side—went to look for vehicles to transport the fighters (if we managed to get them out) and to search for guides to the sewers. We knew that the destruction in the Ghetto was continuing, that every moment was crucial. We met every day to consult and report on our efforts. These meetings included Antek, Zygmunt, sometimes Tadek, and me. And of course Wladka, our landlady, also joined us sometimes. I used to go out in the morning and come back before curfew. I ran around like a maniac with one goal in mind: rescuing the survivors—an impossible mission in those conditions. We contacted some sewer workers and thought the matter was arranged, but at the last minute they decided not to take the risk. No one doubted that getting into the burning Ghetto, while the Germans were systematically destroying all its inhabitants, involved mortal danger.

One evening, after a day of running around, I returned to Wladka's apartment once again empty-handed. It was dark and through the window, in the distance, I saw the burning Ghetto. In despair, I went over everything I had done since we had left the Ghetto; I kept asking myself if I had done everything I could. Unfortunately, we had no one to rely on except ourselves. In my innocence I had thought that by getting out of the Ghetto I had accomplished the essence of my mission; and now I was shocked to find that this wasn't so and that we were still at the very beginning.

As I said, the difficulty was finding a guide through the maze of the sewer tunnels. We assumed we could solve the other problems easily, that we would manage to get hold of vehicles one way or another. We thought we could even find a hiding place in the forests around Warsaw. But how to get the fighters out through the sewers? It had now been five days since I had left the Ghetto. I met with Antek and we had a very difficult conversation. We assessed the situation and concluded that we might be too late. Antek even stated an ultimatum: "If things don't work out, I'm going back to the Ghetto tomorrow." I replied, "If you're thinking of going to the Ghetto through the wall, that's crazy, and you won't do anybody any good. Our comrades there are waiting and counting on us. I would go only if I thought we had a way to rescue them. But if you want to go anyway, you can do it whenever you want." The conversation turned into a shouting match. I remained firm and so did Antek. We parted before curfew. Antek went back to his house on Marszalkowska Street. Apparently he accepted my opinion and gave up the attempt to return to the Ghetto.

In our searches, we were helped by Tadek Shayngut, of Ha-Shomer Ha-Tza'ir, who was already on the Aryan side; by Krzaczek of the PPR (the Polish Workers' party);[46] and also

46. Krzaczek's real name was Wladyslaw Gajek. He was sent by the Gwardia Ludowa, or People's Guard (later the Armia Ludowa), to aid the fighters in the burning Warsaw Ghetto. He helped in the

by the "King of the Blackmailers" (the "Shmaltsovniks"), famous as the leader of the gangs who extorted money from Jews and who helped us—naturally, for a stiff sum. Stefan, the nephew of Anna Wachalska and Maria Sawicka, also helped us. Gradually a plan to get the fighters out of the Ghetto took shape. We needed an exit base where we could descend into the sewers; a guide from the sewer workers; and transportation to take the fighters from the sewer opening to the forest, where they would join a group of comrades who had left the Ghetto through the tunnel to Ogrodowa Street and had been living in the forest since the end of April.[47]

A week later we were prepared to put the plan into action. Krzaczek and Tadek agreed to provide vehicles; they ordered trucks to move furniture to the house next to the sewer exit on Prosta Street. The base from which we would go down to the sewers would be the apartment of the King of the Blackmailers, as he was called on the Aryan side. The king and his "aides" weren't supposed to know we were rescuing Jews, so we concocted this story for them: "A group of Polish Christians went into the Ghetto before the uprising and got stuck there. We are acting on behalf of the AK, and since we now know exactly where the group is, we plan to send men into the Ghetto to get them out."

On the night of May 7, 1943, an advance group went to the Ghetto. To our great disappointment, they soon returned because the sewers were blocked. Moreover, the Germans posted at the sewer exits tossed grenades in and sprayed the

---

rescue operation through the sewers and in taking the fighters to Lomianki Forest (as described below). Later he was exposed as a collaborator with the Polish police.

47. Stefan Grajek (a member of Po'alei Zion Right in Warsaw) and his companions in the Többens-Schultz Area dug a tunnel to Ogrodowa Street and came to the Aryan side at the end of April 1943. See Zuckerman 1993: 364.

sewer with bullets whenever they heard the echo of footsteps. The next night another group was formed, under my
command. My friend Zygmunt refused to come with us for
fear that he wouldn't come back alive this time and that his
little girl, who was with Christians in a village, would be left
alone in the world. So I asked Ryszek to come with us.[48] Ryszek, a friend of Tadek Shayngut, was hiding on the Aryan
side. I knew him well and felt I could rely on him. (Zygmunt
suffered a cruel fate: he was captured a few days later and
shot by the Germans on his way from the village, after visiting his daughter.)

To and from the Ghetto in the Sewers

We set out on May 8. Tadek and Kostek remained outside.
The two sewer workers, Ryszek, and I went in and turned
toward the Ghetto. It was ten o'clock at night and pitch-dark
in the sewers, where there was neither day nor night. Before
we descended into the sewer, the King of the Blackmailers
had begun to suspect I was a Jew and to doubt the truth of
the story about rescuing Christians. I had asked him to post-
pone his investigation of this issue until I came back. We
started walking: the sewer workers first, with me behind.
The central sewer in Warsaw is about two meters high and
the sewage streams in a mighty flow. There is one more difficulty: the side channels are small and we sometimes had
to crawl on our bellies to get through them. It was no pleas-
ure to flounder in excrement, to smell the stench, but we
had no choice. The walking itself went on too long. The
guides changed their minds from time to time and threatened to desert us. I gave them drinks; sometimes I cajoled

48. Ryszek Musselman, born in Warsaw, was a Communist who
served as a liaison between the Polish Workers' party (PPR) on the
Aryan side and the Ghetto. He was killed on May 10, 1943, in the
incident on Prosta Street (see below).

them and sometimes I browbeat them and threatened them with my gun—and thus we advanced. At a certain moment the two men said, "That's it, we're inside the Ghetto." I climbed the iron ladder in the wall of the sewer. Ryszek stayed below to keep the guides from taking off. I lifted the manhole cover and found that we really were in the Ghetto, a few meters away from the gate on Zamenhof Street, between Stawki and Niska. It was two o'clock in the morning.

Zamenhof Street was lighted by a searchlight from Dzika Street. I had to crawl on my belly to Muranowska Street. I had the addresses of a few of our fighting groups. First I made my way to the supply cellar on Franciszkanska Street, where I had left for the Aryan side. I entered the yard but found only the ruins of the shelter. Apparently the Germans had discovered it. Among the ruins I found two men and a woman, not human beings but ghosts. The woman was moaning because her leg was broken. I wanted to take them with me to the Aryan side, but they didn't have the strength to stand up. They told me the ZOB had fought a battle here with a few dozen Germans. It was the battle in which my friend Abraham Eiger had been killed and seventeen-year-old Shlomek Shuster had shown amazing courage.

I left these poor people to their fate and went to Franciszkanska Street 22. I didn't recognize the bunkers in the yard. I signaled with my flashlight, called to the comrades, gave our passwords. Suddenly a woman's voice rose from the ruins to lead me to where our comrades were hiding. She told me her leg was broken and asked me to look for her in the heap of debris. I walked around for about half an hour, trying to follow her voice, but it came from a different place every time, as if in a mirage. I sensed that time was running out. I stopped searching. In despair, I rushed to Nalewki, Mila, and Zamenhof streets, but I didn't find anyone anywhere. The Ghetto had been completely burned down. Piles of corpses rolled around in the streets, in the yards, and among the heaps of ruins.

A sudden calm surrounded me. I felt so good among the ruins of the Ghetto, near the corpses that were dear to me, that I wanted to stay and wait for dawn, for the Germans to come, to kill some of them and then die. My life passed dizzily before my eyes, like a film. I saw myself fall in battle as the last Jew in the Warsaw Ghetto. I felt I was on the border between sanity and madness.

With a superhuman effort, I wrenched myself free of thoughts of suicide and decided to return to the sewers. The closer I got to the manhole cover, the brighter were the searchlights in the area because the German position was close to the entrance of the Ghetto. I crawled the last part of the way and finally managed to slither into the sewer. I went down and closed the cover. "Let's go! There's nobody there!" The shout leaped out of my mouth. It wasn't my voice, it wasn't a human voice: it was aimed at Ryszek and the sewer workers who were waiting for me.

We started back. As we walked I signaled with my flashlight, in case someone remained hiding here. Suddenly I heard a noise in a side sewer. I thought I could make out a flickering light. Were they Germans or Jews? My nerves were stretched to the limit, my finger caressed the trigger of my revolver. I was ready to shoot, but something stopped me. I waited and repeated the password of the organization. The tension mounted. From the side sewer a group of ten fighters suddenly burst out. For a moment we were petrified. Was this a dream? Everyone wanted to hug me. A few minutes later I knew we had arrived only one day late. . . .[49]

On the spot, I sent two of that group back to the Ghetto to round up the remnants of the fighters and bring them to

49. Tuvia Borzykowski also described this incident; see Borzykowski 1972: 102.

the sewer. One of them was my best friend, Shlomo Shuster, my comrade-in-arms in the Brushmakers' Area; we had been inseparable until I left for the Aryan side. I gave the fighters clear instructions: "When you come back from the Ghetto, stay together in the sewer, as close as possible to the exit." I emphasized that they were absolutely not to disperse into the side sewers. I promised to lead the way and even to post fighters to guide them at junctions where they might get lost. On the way our comrades told what had happened to them and described the eight days I had been out of the Ghetto. The shelter at Mila 18 had not been discovered until the day of May 8. The bunker had been surrounded and when the Germans had found the ventilating slits, they had poured poison gas into them. Almost a hundred members of the Jewish Fighting Organization had been gathered in the bunker, led by Mordechai Anielewicz, the commander. Hungry, broken, hopeless, some of the fighters had committed suicide; others had tried to break out and had fallen dead at the entrance to the bunker.

Before leaving the sewer, I once more briefed those who remained below. Over and over I emphasized the need to keep from scattering and to maintain total silence so as not to be discovered. Finally, I promised to make contact in the afternoon, before curfew. We kept walking, as the water came up to our waist.

Then Ryszek and I climbed out of the sewers. Tadek and Krzaczek were waiting for us at the home of the "King of the Blackmailers." We changed clothes and went to our comrades to report on the situation. We decided that Tadek and I would contact the fighters in the sewers at dusk. Krzaczek was assigned to get hold of a vehicle to take the fighters to the forest. We agreed to meet the next day, May 10, right after curfew, at the manhole cover and to take out the fighters gathered below.

At the Manhole on Prosta Street

At five o'clock the next morning we were standing at the manhole cover on Prosta Street, waiting for Tadek and the trucks Krzaczek was supposed to obtain. He was to call a moving company to send a truck to take some furniture to a house near the manhole. We were to force the driver at gunpoint to take the fighters coming out of the sewer to their destination. Tadek worked with Krzaczek to get the truck. By nine o'clock no one had come back, and there was no truck either. It was very dangerous to bring the comrades out of the sewer at that hour. On the other hand, if we didn't bring them out soon, we were condemning them to death. So I decided we had to get them out that day whenever we could. It would have been good to have an armed cover during the exit, but unfortunately we didn't.

Another hour passed before the truck arrived with Kostek and other "Aryan-looking" fellows: Jurek, Ryszek, and Wacek. We surrounded the manhole cover because, at the corner of Zelazna Street, about a hundred meters away, was the German-Ukrainian guard, the guard of the "small Ghetto." We opened the manhole cover. I didn't recognize any of those coming out: figures from another world, ghosts, yet I knew every one of them! I covered the exit, Krzaczek sat in the driver's seat, the rest of us helped the fighters out of the sewer. Meanwhile, Israel Kanal, the commander of the Central Ghetto, shouted to me from the truck, "Kazik, is there cover here?"[50] And I yelled back, "Everybody around," point-

---

50. Israel Kanal, born in Bydgoszcz, was active in Akiba and infiltrated the Jewish police in the Ghetto. One of the first ZOB fighters, he fought in the January Uprising and was commander of the Central Ghetto in the April Uprising. Afterward he came to the Aryan side through the sewers. In October 1943 he was deported to Auschwitz, where he was killed at about 22 years of age.

ing to the big group of onlookers gathered at the manhole cover. One of them joked, "The cats are coming out."

Meanwhile, I came on a Polish police officer on his way to the German guard. I went up to him and politely but firmly explained that this was an operation of the Polish underground and that he would do better to go back where he came from and pretend he hadn't seen a thing. The man obeyed without a word. We went on taking the people out. More than half an hour passed—complete victory. Terrified, I continued walking around in the crowd of onlookers, which increased by the minute. Suddenly I noticed that they had stopped taking people out of the sewers. I rushed to the manhole cover to find out what had happened. "It looks like there aren't any more fighters down there," Ryszek said to me. I bent down into the the sewer and roared, "Anybody inside?" Not a sound. I ordered the manhole cover closed, and as I went to the driver's cab, I told Krzaczek we had to move. In the back of the truck were more than thirty comrades. I got in. As the truck began to move, Zivia ordered me to stop because several comrades were still left in a side sewer. I refused. I said I was the commander of the operation and that it wouldn't be right or wise to delay because the Germans were close and were liable to show up any minute. I added that the truck was completely full; another truck which had been ordered hadn't come. After we took those people to the forest, we'd come back and try to find those who were left.

We went on to Lomianki Forest. I remained standing in the truck. Krzaczek was sitting next to the driver. We had to pass through the whole city and cross the bridge over the Wisla. From time to time I ordered preparations in case we were stopped by German patrols. When we got to the bridge, I saw that vehicles were being stopped and searched by the Germans. At the last minute Krzaczek ordered the driver to turn around, which he did with a screech. We tried our luck

on another bridge and succeeded in crossing without incident. When we got to the forest, where there was a group of
fighters from the Többens-Schultz Area, Zivia came up and
said she wanted to shoot me. I replied, "No problem. We can
settle our accounts immediately. I'll shoot you and you'll
shoot me and we'll be even."

Zivia was angry and tense. She told me that Shlomek and
Adolf had been sent to call the comrades in the side sewer
as soon as the manhole cover had been removed, and had
promised to wait for them. I couldn't help or comfort Zivia.
The night before I had dropped a note into the sewer telling
everyone to be ready to leave before dawn the next day. I had
carefully explained to Shlomek that he was not to scatter the
people, and I had also gotten confirmation that all of them
were ready to be evacuated. I fell into a depression. I had to
stay in Lomianki with the comrades and escort them to a
safe place, since nobody else wanted to stay with them, despite my request. So we agreed they'd go back where we came
out and see what could still be done.

Many years have passed. Much has been told and written
about that group coming out from the sewers. Later I discussed it with Marek Edelman, who was one of those rescued. He was walking next to Zivia. When they came to the
manhole cover, the two of them went from the end of the
group to the head of the line, where they had to make the
decisions. They received the note I had dropped telling them
of the postponement of the escape till the next day because
we hadn't yet found trucks. Marek told me, "I was the one
who promised Shlomek and Adolf when they went to look
for the 'lost' group in the junctions of the sewer that we
wouldn't leave without them. While Zivia said, 'I promised
them.' "[51] And I have told how furious she was when I ordered the truck to move.

51. See Edelman's account in Krall 1986: 76.

It's hard to know why they delayed. The real story was lost with them when they were killed.

Ryszek, Jurek, and Wacek returned to town in the truck. They went to rescue the rest of the group, in the hope that they had reached the manhole cover on Prosta Street. I waited for them to come back—one hour, two hours, three hours. No one returned. I started worrying; every minute that passed increased the anxiety gnawing at me. I decided I had to do something. I left the forest for Warsaw. As I passed near Bank Square, from the tram I saw people gathering on the street. Impelled by some instinct, I jumped off the moving tram and made my way through the crowd. Then I saw Ryszek lying dead on the pavement. Not far from him I saw Jurek, also killed. Germans and police were crowded in the square.

I mingled with the crowd and listened. Apparently, some Jews had burst out of the sewer. The German guard had been no more than a hundred meters from the manhole, and when they had sensed something suspicious, they had approached and opened fire. They had shot those coming up to the street as well as those inside the sewer. There had been a struggle and every last one of the Jews had been killed.

Later, we heard more: a Polish woman who had seen Jurek and Ryszek in the first rescue operation identified them when they returned from the forest to the manhole cover and turned them over to the Germans. The two were shot on the spot.

Obviously, I had to get away immediately, since I was liable to be identified as one of those walking around in charge of things. And I did get away before the Germans spotted me.

The next day I met Antek, told him about the incident with Zivia, and listed the names of the fighters we had rescued. I said that Zivia was among them, and I sensed that it was hard for him to believe it. We made an appointment for the next day to go to Lomianki to visit our comrades. The rules of caution sometimes prevented us from making quick contact. Frequently, each of us had to make serious decisions on our own. We went to Lomianki the next day as planned. We took food for our comrades and made our way without incident. At the edge of the forest we came on an advance guard of fighters, who led us in. We spent several hours with the fighters and, after meeting the surviving command staff of the organization and Antek, we returned to Warsaw at dusk.

4 On the Aryan Side

After the Rescue Operation

Lomianki is the name of a small town and a forest, called Puszcza Kampinowska in Polish. In mid-May 1943, comrades who had come out of the Ghetto in the early days of the uprising were hiding there. We knew it wasn't an ideal hiding place, but we didn't have anything better. My efforts were now devoted mainly to seeking another hiding place for the fighters, and soon afterward they were moved, some to forests around Wyszków, others to clandestine apartments in and around Warsaw. I also tended to those who came out of the Ghetto hungry, almost naked, and in bad health. We had to provide them with clothing and, especially and immediately, with food.

On that first visit to the comrades with Antek, one of the important things we brought them was a few lemons. It was very hard to get lemons during the war; you had to buy them in various places on the black market and gather enough for dozens of comrades who needed them. People who had stayed in bunkers and absorbed smoke felt bad, and sucking lemons made them feel better. They wanted lemons and we filled their request.

Once I spent the night in the forest, but I couldn't sleep because it was too cold. We didn't have proper clothes or blankets. We kept each other warm and somehow the night passed. At dawn we did calisthenics to warm up, if only a little. We got in touch with a peasant in the village of Lomianki whom we called "Chlop" (Polish for peasant), a good-hearted and warm soul who agreed to supply food to our comrades. We would give him money and he would buy food in various places so as not to make the shopkeepers suspicious. In the evening he would hitch his horse to his wagon and bring them the food. He always added something to drink, sometimes hot soup he made himself. With the help of his children, he would bring the food and hot soup to the forest, and would warn the group when he heard that the Germans were planning a search. He was our source of information on what was happening. He once said there were rumors and whispers in the village about a group of Jews in the forest. The situation deteriorated and we were afraid the Gestapo would find out. During their stay in Lomianki, one of our comrades died of weakness and perhaps from the effects of poisoned gas he had breathed in the sewers.[52] He had to be buried on the spot, and the peasant lent them spades and other tools to dig the grave.

As I said, Lomianki wasn't a large forest and it was very hard to hide there. Obviously, it could serve only as a temporary hiding place, and we had to look for another as soon as possible. We moved some of our companions, like Zivia, Tuvia Borzykowski, and Marek Edelman, to hiding places in Warsaw. We hesitated, not sure if it was better to be in a partisan group in the forest or hiding in an apartment in Warsaw. However, Zivia and Marek were members of the command staff and had to be accessible and available for meetings at any time. Zivia, Marek, and Tuvia were taken to an apartment at Komitetowa Street 4, where Antek and I were living.

After making contact with the Polish underground, which gave orders to its members in the field, most of the fighters were taken to the forest in Wyszków. You couldn't be on the Aryan side without identity documents. While the comrades were in Lomianki, the Polish underground had helped me get a *Kennkarte* (the identity card issued by the Germans in the

52. Yehuda Wengrower, a member of Ha-Shomer Ha-Tza'ir. According to Zivia Lubetkin, he had been unable to bear the thirst in the sewers and had drunk water from the gutter. He died at age 23, the day after the fighters reached Lomianki.

Generalgouvernement which replaced the Polish identity documents).[53] I was sent to the office of a church in one of the Warsaw suburbs. I went to the clerk and requested a birth certificate (which was required in order to receive the Kennkarte). They had coached me in what to say. This was a document whose real owner, someone my age, was no longer alive. The clerk looked at me sharply and spat out: "Funny world—one person dies and another walks around and impersonates him." I didn't say anything. He asked my address, the names of my parents, and the other details of questionnaires everywhere in the world. I answered briefly and finally got the birth certificate.

From there I went to the registration office where Poles worked with Germans, and submitted a proper request for a Kennkarte. My fingerprints were taken like any other Polish citizen's. At the end of this process I had a Kennkarte in the name of Antoni-Julian Ksiezopolski—a common name among the Polish aristocracy. At the same time I got a forged Kennkarte from the Polish underground in another name. I kept the document with the name Ksiezopolski with me, while the other one was kept at "home" in case of trouble. (Incidentally, not long ago, I got the work card of Irena Gelblum, a ZOB courier and friend of "Green Marysia."[54] To my surprise, I discovered that at that time, on the Aryan side, Irena adopted "my" last name—Ksiezopolski. As Marysia says, she explained at the time that she felt safer being "related" to me.)

53. The Generalgouvernement was the administrative district created by the Nazi authorities in central Poland, including Krakow and Warsaw.

54. "Green Marysia" (Luba Gewisser) was born in Warsaw in 1924 and left the Ghetto during the Great Aktsia in the summer of 1942. She worked as a ZOB courier on the Aryan side and now lives in Tel Aviv.

From the Aryan side we kept track of what was going on in the Ghetto. Every single day we heard shooting. The Ghetto was still burning. Here and there we saw smoke rising; the smell of singed flesh permeated the whole district abutting the burning area. Sometimes you could distinguish between German shots and the shots of the last of the Jews, since those left in the Ghetto mostly used pistols, while the German army used machine guns and heavy weapons. We assumed that ZOB groups were still operating in the Ghetto, but there was no way to get in touch with them. A last attempt to make contact was on May 9, 1943, when I sent Shlomo Shuster and another comrade to the Ghetto to gather up the remaining fighters. Rumors were circulating that groups of fighters were still operating among the ruins—and the shooting we heard confirmed them.

Life on the Aryan side of Warsaw went on as usual. Every day I would walk through the streets of the city, and some invisible force drew me to the walls of the Ghetto, an inexplicable longing to see the Ghetto as the fire was still destroying parts of it. I felt free but helpless. I would glance at the faces of the people passing by the Ghetto walls; everyone hurried on his way and about his business, no one paid much attention to what was happening on the other side of the walls. I had to pretend so as not to be discovered. Since every careless wink was liable to give me away, I had to be careful not to express any sympathy or grief. It took me weeks to get used to the idea that the Ghetto no longer existed for me.

Every time I walked around the walls, I would go back to what I was doing. Most of the wall remained standing, although there were breaches here and there. I didn't hear any expressions of sympathy from the Poles about what was happening to the Jews of their city; some of them even seemed happy about the "purification" of Warsaw's Jews.

To pretend all the time, not to identify yourself to anyone—that's not easy to live with. I was often gripped by a strong desire to confess. In general it isn't easy to step into someone else's shoes, to project a borrowed image, the image of a Pole. "Antoni-Julian Ksiezopolski, parents' names so-and-so, family included X number of persons, born in . . . "— I recited these details to myself over and over. If someone had woken me up in the middle of the night, I could have quoted "my pedigree" by heart. The first time I allowed myself to say something in favor of the Jews again was during the Polish Uprising in 1944.

In August or September 1943, a survivor from the Ghetto came to us on the Aryan side. I don't remember how we made contact with him. The man told about a group of some twenty Jews who were alive and hiding in the debris. He said their situation was awful and they had kept alive for several weeks on a few potatoes they had found in a cellar full of burned potatoes. They soaked them in water for a day and divided the "dish" into one portion a day per person.

An acquaintance of mine, a Polish policeman, agreed to help rescue the group from the Ghetto on a fixed date. Since policemen were allowed to walk around after curfew, we could get one of our men into the Ghetto in the evening. We decided that if anyone asked whom he was taking, he would answer that he had arrested the man—or men—and was taking them to the nearest police station. Things went according to plan. We managed to get the group out and the policeman brought them to a temporary hiding place at Mokotowska Street 1, where I met them. They were exhausted. Despite their hunger, we were careful not to give them too much food because we knew it might kill them. We didn't have experts in caring for starving people, but we did know that you had to be careful to give them small portions. Even so, some died, apparently from overeating.

It turned out that they had come together by chance and had taken cover together in the Ghetto, where they held out for some time. They told me about German operations in the

Ghetto. This was after General Stroop announced officially that the Ghetto was *Judenrein* (purified of Jews), and in fact that wasn't far from the truth: only a few individuals were hiding here and there.[55]

The Germans used Jews from Hungary and Greece to bury the dead so epidemics wouldn't spread in the city, something they were mortally afraid of. The Jews were also used to gather property left in the Ghetto, work that went on almost until the beginning of the Polish Uprising.[56] These Jews were lodged in Pawiak Prison, which had formerly been inside the Ghetto. Later I will tell how we contacted two of the prisoners who escaped to the Aryan side.

To picture the situation at that time, you must understand the Ghetto as part of the city of Warsaw. The municipal government and its branches were responsible for the normal functioning of that area. What had previously been the "small Ghetto" became a residential area, rented out by city hall. Here, in the heart of the city, was a big mass of nothing but ruins, obstructed streets, and bunkers filled with corpses. Even a normal government would have had trouble dealing with such a situation. During the Polish Uprising there was no fighting in the area of the Ghetto. The Polish rebels fought in other quarters of the city.

With Antek

I had heard of Antek even before I met him. The first time I saw him in person was during his visit to the base of Benjamin Wald's fighting group on Leszno Street. He made a "commander's visit" there, asked questions, was interested in

55. Gen. Jürgen Stroop commanded the German forces that put down the revolt in the Warsaw Ghetto. His report of May 16, 1943, which included daily accounts of battles and photographs, was titled: "The Warsaw Ghetto Is No More" (see References).

56. In August 1944.

events, patted us on the shoulder, made remarks. I was impressed by the way he looked: tall, erect, with a mustache—he looked important. Our next meeting was on the Aryan side, where I went on a mission from the ZOB command staff to find how to get the fighters out of the collapsing Ghetto. I reported to Antek on the progress of the uprising in the Ghetto and said that the fighters expected to be rescued. We sketched a plan of operations for the near future. When I realized that we wouldn't get much help from the Polish underground and that we had to rely on ourselves, we divided the tasks between us, aware that it would take a tremendous effort to organize the rescue. Perhaps more than the others, I understood that we couldn't lose a single moment, that every delay might seal the fate of our companions in the Ghetto.

After our friends had been safely brought out of the Ghetto to the Lomianki Forest, I met with Antek every day, and sometimes we would spend whole days together. For several months the two of us lived alone at Wolska Street 6. Every day we planned our activities for that day. Our basic mission was to establish contact with the remnants of the Jews throughout the Generalgouvernement. We used the communications network wherever possible, either in the remaining ghettoes or in the labor camps. We made contact with our people in Koniecpol near Czestochowa, in Plaszów, Poniatów, Trawniki, the HASAG camp in Czestochowa, and in a camp in Skarzysko-Kamienna.[57] In addition, we established contact with Jews hiding in and around Warsaw. We would bring them money, forged documents, and underground publications.

Antek and I would go out to the street together in the

57. A partisan base was established in Koniecpol in 1943 by ZOB member Yehuda Glikstein. HASAG Pelzerei (acronym for Hugo Schneider Aktiengesellschaft) was a forced labor camp for the manufacture of munitions. For details, see Ainsztein 1974: 818–822.

morning; then each of us went his own way. In the evening we would meet and report to each other on the situation. We held these meetings while walking in the streets, in parks, or sitting in cafés.

Antek's work was primarily to maintain contact with the members of the Polish underground and with the Jewish leaders hiding in Warsaw. He maintained contact simultaneously with the two Polish undergrounds: the Armia Krajowa (AK) and the Armia Ludowa (AL). The AL knew about our contacts with the AK, whereas the AK was not supposed to know about our contacts with the AL.

The division of labor was clear. Antek was now the commander of the ZOB throughout Poland. I was considered his right hand, and in many places the head courier of the ZOB on the Aryan side of Warsaw. I know that sometimes, when he didn't want to praise me to my face, he would define our relations in typical "Antek" language: "Kazik was the only one who always knew where I was at every hour of the day and night. Even Zivia didn't know that." His Vilna Polish accent was liable to give him away, since it was easy to spot that he wasn't from Warsaw, whereas I was a typical Warsaw kid and my Polish dialect was common in the big city. When we walked together in the streets, it was understood and agreed that he wasn't the spokesman. I would run errands for him and set up secret meetings with our people as well as with members of the Polish underground. We couriers demonstrated great enterprise and agility in creating contacts for our "bosses." We had our own methods. It was a severe blow for Antek when his personal courier, Franya Beatus, committed suicide at the height of the Ghetto Uprising, and he was profoundly depressed.

Luba (called "Green Marysia") told me that when the Ghetto was burning, she and Irena would sit in their apartment at Panska Street 5, looking out from the top-floor window. They could see the flames clearly and hear the shots.

Antek would come to the apartment and the three of them would sit facing the fire, listening to the sounds and weeping.

In such conditions, regular meetings of the ZOB command staff naturally weren't held. They were only called from time to time for members of the staff who were still alive. In fact, I was a full participant in those deliberations since, except for anything having to do with history and the archives, they concerned issues that involved me, as one who either carried operations out or assigned them to others.

I took on various missions and errands. We couriers tried to carry out these missions without an escort, and only rarely, when circumstances demanded it, was I accompanied by anyone. Our tasks were:

1. maintaining contact with people in the camps and ghettoes; preserving this contact between them and free Jews—who were in touch with the Polish underground and knew what was going on in the world and on the front—was important and encouraging.
2. delivering money and financial assistance to various branches of the organization.
3. delivering forged documents.
4. delivering underground publications.
5. supplying weapons to places where uprisings were planned and prepared.

ZOB couriers carried these missions out throughout the occupation. When a specific mission was assigned, we always weighed carefully who had the best chance of performing it. My work wasn't courier work in the narrow sense, since I would often both initiate the activity and carry it out. In fact, I was Antek's deputy, and in that role I had to make decisions required by the circumstances at any given moment.

I would go from place to place to meet and talk with people in hiding. Thus, I was involved with acquiring weapons and transferring them to the places of fighting, for example, to Czestochowa. I was often helped in this by our women couriers and by Gentiles who were willing to risk their lives on such errands. Some of those whom I sent on these missions were Luba, Irena, Marysia Sawicka (a Pole), the Jewish Marysia (called "Blue-Eyed Marysia"), Inka,[58] a Jewish fellow named Natek, a Polish policeman (whom I've already mentioned) named Adamczyk, sometimes the young son of Felek Rajszczak, and others.

Contacts in Czestochowa

As I recall, it was in June 1943 that a fellow called Lala (Yitzhak Windman) came from Czestochowa to Warsaw. I learned that he was one of the ZOB survivors in that city. I met him in a place determined in advance, and he gave me a detailed report of what had happened there. The most important thing he had come to ask for was weapons, because they were planning to revolt. We agreed to get hold of as many weapons for them as we could gather in a short time.

Lala asked if we could go to a place where we could view the Ghetto. As we approached the wall, we were assailed by blackmailers trying to extort money from us. Those human scum intuitively recognized even those Jews who looked "Aryan." I saw a group of people starting to whisper among themselves and pointing at us. I had time to tell Lala to remain calm and not to try to run away. I told him that I had a gun and that he could count on me to deal with the situation; the most important thing was not to panic. After we walked on a bit, I said, "Lala, we're walking to the tram. Don't look back and don't show any nervousness." We

58. Inka Szwajger was a physician and author of *I Remember Nothing More: The Warsaw Children's Hospital and the Jewish Resistance* (1990). She lived in Poland after the war and died in March 1993.

stopped at the station with the whole group on our tail. Before we got on the tram, they caught up with us, pointed to Lala, and said: "He's a Jew." I laughed and replied: "If he's a Jew, come on, we'll take care of him together." I signaled to Lala to keep walking behind me. We boarded the tram with the group right behind us. As the tram moved away, Lala's nerves seemed to give out and he jumped off. Some of the blackmailers noticed and jumped off after him, while the others continued on with me. I got off at the next stop, but Lala had vanished. The blackmailers stuck to me, and I decided to settle accounts with them at the first opportunity. I went on walking a long time, striding confidently, not looking back. I stopped at a display window to find out if the group was still behind me. Apparently, they had concluded that I was a "legitimate Pole" and had disappeared. Later I was told that Lala had indeed been nabbed by the blackmailers, who stole everything he had on him, beat him, and finally left him alone.

If something kept you from a meeting, it was understood that you would go back to the meeting place, or to some other place determined in advance, to make a new contact. So I went back to the same place at the determined time for three days in a row, but Lala didn't show up. I was worried, but there was nothing more I could do. Later I learned that he had managed to get back to Czestochowa. I wanted to tell our companions there not to send him back to Warsaw anymore, in case he was be identified again. Later I learned that Lala had nevertheless been sent to Warsaw again. On the way, he had been robbed and killed, or turned over to the Germans, apparently by Krzaczek.

I started gathering weapons for our companions in Czestochowa. In those days Zivia, Antek, Marek Edelman, and I took part in meetings of the ZOB command staff. We lived in the same apartment. At one of the meetings, it was decided that I would go to Czestochowa to make direct contact with the remaining members of the halutz youth movement there. I was to meet them in the village of Koniecpol, where they were hiding in a peasant's barn. I had to find them without asking the villagers where they were. I was given directions in advance, although I don't remember by whom—most likely by Lala when he was in Warsaw.

I had to take the train from Warsaw, get off at the station near Koniecpol, and continue on foot. Passengers were searched as they got on and off the trains—young people were sent to work in Germany. Fortunately for me, the trip went without incident. I came to Koniecpol and went straight to the peasant's house. I tried to chat with him, to sense if I really had come to the right address. After groping around in conversation, I concluded that I was indeed in the right place, especially because of the nervousness I discerned in the eyes of the inhabitants of the house. I tried to convince them that I had come from Warsaw especially to see the young Jews hiding on the farm. I explained that I had come to help, but the peasant stuck with his refusal and kept claiming that he didn't know what I was talking about. After a while, I started to wonder whether I had indeed come to the right address and whether I should go on pressing the man. I decided to try another approach I don't know why, but instead of telling the peasant I knew the Jews were in the barn, I got up and started walking there. It was my behavior that convinced him, and he led me to our friends.

The Jews were stunned when, through the slits, they saw a stranger coming toward the barn, which was nothing but a straw shed. They didn't know me and I didn't know them. I was dressed like a Gestapo agent. I dressed like that deliberately, in a long black-leather coat, visored cap, and boots. I adopted the way of walking, the style of talking, the appearance, and outward behavior of a Gestapo agent. Germans weren't the only ones who served in the Gestapo, whose

ranks included members of other nationalities, including
Jews.[59] I took a considerable risk in walking like that to the
barn, since the group was armed and, if their nerves had given
out, they might have opened fire on me. I went into the barn
and found our companions hiding in a corner. It took only a
few minutes for us to begin talking freely. They were very
happy about making direct contact with the ZOB. Zivia and
Antek were familiar figures to them. I brought them underground newspapers and money, and we arranged to continue
communicating. I came to them at dusk and must have
stayed overnight.

After returning to Warsaw, I got busy acquiring weapons
for the Jews. I decided that the best way to transport them
was with the help of the Polish policeman Adamczyk. I had
known him personally before the war, when he had been a
customer in my parents' store. Now, on the Aryan side, I met
him accidentally on the street. A feeling in my heart told me
to try to recruit him for our operations, despite my friends'
worries. He invited me to his home and I felt him out in
conversation, hinting at my connections with the AK. He
didn't let me down. One of the first missions I assigned to
him was to transport weapons (pistols and bullets) to the
group of Jews, thus largely reducing the danger. He performed
his task loyally and efficiently. He didn't do it for money but
solely for humanitarian motives. The only payments he got
from us were travel expenses and money for the work day he
gave up for our errand.

Contact with our friends in Czestochowa became more
regular— almost weekly instead of once every three months.
We fixed proper rules of access and identification to prevent

59. For instances of Jews who collaborated with the Gestapo, see
Zuckerman (1993: 63ff., 441–445).

what might have happened, God forbid, when I had dropped in on them the first time as a complete surprise.

I maintained contact with Adamczyk until the Polish Uprising. Then he disappeared and we lost track of him. He was a human being—and that wasn't a simple thing in those days.

5 Clandestine Apartments

The Apartment at Komitetowa 4 Is "Burned"

The apartment at Komitetowa Street 4 had once belonged to one Jewish family and was now inhabited by another. The supposed tenant went by the name of Stasia Kopik and lived with her three daughters and the husband of one of the daughters. When she rented the apartment, Stasia introduced herself to the landlord and the porter as the wife of a Polish officer who had been taken prisoner. She was blond and spoke perfect Polish. So did her daughter Zosia, who also looked like a Gentile.[60] The other members of the family lived in hiding there: in one of the rooms a bookshelf was set up, dividing the open part of the room from the hidden part.

Antek and I also lived in the apartment. We weren't registered as tenants and, for the sake of appearances, we pretended to be guests of the mother and daughter. Antek was "visiting" the mother and I the daughter. A few leaders of the movement had been brought from Lomianki Forest. Zivia, Marek Edelman, Tuvia Borzykowski, and a few other companions were living there.

One day Gestapo agents came to the apartment, examined the documents of the two women living there officially, asked them some more questions, and even searched. Apparently everything looked all right to them since, when they had finished looking around, they left. At that moment I came through the gate, not knowing who was in the apart-

60. In fact, Stasia Kopek and her daughter Zosia were Jews. Her husband had been killed in the Ghetto during the Great Aktsia in the summer of 1942, and the two women had escaped to the Aryan side.

ment. The Gestapo visit made us uncomfortable and anxious. Was it a sign of a denunciation?

We started thinking about moving to another apartment. One day a Christian woman, one of the tenants of the building, came to our apartment and said straight out that she knew Jews were hiding there. She added that the women of the house were also almost certainly Jews. She came right to the point and hinted that, for a handsome sum, she would keep her mouth shut. We made an appointment with her to settle the issue. We considered the place "burned" and decided to clear out.

I came to meet the woman with Natek. We agreed that after we got out of her all she knew about the apartment and its tenants, we'd weigh the risk—and then decide what to do. The meeting was held at dusk. We started talking as we walked. Suddenly, disregarding our plan and without any warning, Natek pulled out a gun and shot the woman. The bullet whistled past my ear but didn't hit her. Natek ran away and I had no choice but to finish what he had started, which I did with two pistol shots. I immediately fled in a panic—I didn't have time to see if the woman was hit and had fallen. As I ran, I roared out, "The Germans are hunting people, watch out!" The people in the street started dispersing, which made it easier for me to escape. When I got to the apartment on Panska Street, I sat down to clean my pistol, only to discover that the two bullets were stuck in the barrel and hadn't fired. I can't say I regretted it.[61]

The official tenant of the apartment on Komitetowa Street went on living there unharmed, while we moved to another apartment, at Panska Street 5. It was rented in the names of two of our comrades who were posing as Christians, Luba Gewisser ("Green Marysia") and Irena Gelblum (Irka). These

61. Zuckerman tells a slightly different version of this incident; see Zuckerman 1993: 430–432.

two young belles were an integral part of the Polish population of Warsaw. Luba's boyfriend, Jurek Grossberg, one of the
leaders of the Polish Scouts, was hiding in the apartment. He
was a student who had good contacts in patriotic Polish cir-
cles (the Scouts were known as "lovers of their homeland and
mother tongue"). But every rose has a thorn: the man looked
like a typical Jew, and his appearance was liable to give him
away.

Luba had rented the apartment even before the Ghetto Uprising, and Antek and I would often drop by there. Even during the war it was hardly unusual for young men to visit two
young women. The neighbors were even interested in the
"affairs" of the two belles and could identify the "lover" of
each one of them. As I said, Antek and I were the first suitors,
but other comrades—including Tadek (Tuvia Shayngut)—
also came. A few times, Tadek hid weapons there to be sent
to our comrades in some ghetto.

We brought Zivia, Marek, Tuvia Borzykowski, and Krysia
to this apartment, and Antek and I also moved in.[62] The fact
that the two of us came and went openly explained to the
neighbors the relatively large quantities of food the girls
bought—much more food than they needed for themselves.

Panska Street 5: Apartment and Operations Base

Before the Great Aktsia in the Warsaw Ghetto, Panska Street
was one of the streets of the "small Ghetto." After the Ghetto
was reduced, the entire zone became an "Aryan" area. The
municipal government established a special office to tend to
the empty apartments; some of them had been partly destroyed, others completely, but all had been "cleansed" of
Jews and their possessions. The intention was to rent the
apartments again, this time to Poles.

62. Krysia (Sara Biderman) was a ZOB courier on the Aryan side
of Warsaw. She lived at Miodowa Street 24.

For us in the ZOB, an apartment in the Aryan section wasn't simply a house and a hiding place; it was also a base, with arms caches, where we held meetings and training exercises—a base for launching underground operations. The chronicles of the ZOB survivors can be told by the order of the apartments they lived in; these were like milestones and chronological tables. We were dispersed in several apartments at the same time. If we could easily have acquired clandestine apartments, we would certainly have rented more of them. At any rate, as I recall, the apartment at Panska 5 was special. It was in a standard three- or four-story apartment building. There were two apartments on the top floor, one of which was rented by Luba. The building was on a typical street, with pedestrians coming and going. This was wartime, but the front was still remote and life went on almost normally, within the constraints of the occupation. The door to the apartment was opened from inside only after the agreed-upon signal was knocked: taaa-ta-ta-ta.

People who looked Jewish, like Zivia, Marek, Tuvia, and Jurek, didn't go out at all. Whenever a guest came to the apartment who wasn't in on the secret, or some stranger, like the man who came to read the electric meter, the mailman, or a neighbor to borrow something—everyone had to hide immediately in a hiding place where there was barely room to move. The people who were confined to the apartment maintained contact with the outside world through those of us who looked Aryan. In time, a gap developed between those of us who were house-bound and those who "walked around freely." Despite the danger I faced when I walked around the streets of Warsaw or when I met members of the Polish underground or Jews in cafés, I felt freer than my friends who weren't allowed out. All their information was filtered through us and they had no direct impressions of their own. Antek and I, on the other hand, left in the morning, came back before curfew, and spent most of our time outside to give an impression that we were going to work. Luba and Irena would go to work like other Poles and come home before us.

Because of this continual friction, dissension and arguments arose more readily between the two women and the people confined to the apartment than between those in hiding and Antek and me. Keep in mind that the people in that apartment had come together by chance and were forced to live together twenty-four hours a day. Luba and Irena had a different background than the rest of us, since they hadn't been members of the Zionist youth movement. Zivia was eight or nine years older than they and was well known in the Zionist movement and among the Jews. Antek and I would come back tired from our day's work and usually reported on what we had done that day. Zivia was a good cook and we all ate dinner together. The standard menu was potato soup and horsemeat.

For a long time we debated the issue of carrying weapons. My comrades argued that we mustn't carry them in the street because of the danger of falling into the hands of a German patrol and being arrested. My opinion was that we shouldn't walk around without weapons because every encounter with the Germans could get us turned over to the Gestapo, and that had to be prevented at all costs. Once during an argument, with my gun in my pocket, I apparently held my finger on the trigger. A shot went off and the bullet hit the floor, grazing the sole of my shoe.

After one stormy fight between Antek and me about the way to carry out our work (I can't recall the details), I was very offended and decided to go on "strike." The strike didn't last long, and I went back to work a day or two later, after we agreed that I would do things as I saw fit.

Our conversations covered various subjects. One that con-

cerned us very much was what would happen after the war,
if we survived. We tried to imagine what would happen when
the war ended, since everything comes to an end sometime.
How would things look? I don't think we actually believed
we'd survive. Only at times would such an idea creep into
our hearts, and then we'd talk about what we'd do and try to
imagine how other people would treat us. We also raised the
issue of how we should treat the Germans. These were the
thoughts of young people who had experienced more than
their share of suffering at the hands of the Germans. Each of
us had a different opinion about what to do when the war
was over. Unlike the rest of my comrades, I argued that we
should devote ourselves to taking revenge on the Germans. I
had a vague idea that, just as we had organized for the Ghetto
Uprising, we now had to make a plan to take revenge on the
Germans. My plan was to set up a large-scale revenge operation and kill a great many Germans, especially SS men and
Gestapo agents. I was willing to go even further and say that
we should take revenge on the whole German nation. In that
period we hadn't yet heard of a "good German" and I saw the
German people as my sworn enemies, willing to do everything to annihilate us. I firmly believed that, if we survived,
we had to kill as many Germans as we could. We sat and
argued, and the debate was often heated. These were emotional issues, since a big question-mark hovered over our
lives and our survival. Even then, Zivia and Antek rejected
the idea of revenge. Their decided opinion was always that
at the end of the war we had to immigrate to Eretz Israel and
to follow the commandments of the Zionist movement. We
thrashed this subject out in many conversations and never
came to a conclusion.

Aside from these arguments, I would like to tell you
briefly about my love affairs. I've already mentioned Dvora
Baran. As long as a human being is alive, even with inade-

quate food and in the most difficult conditions, "this world" doesn't come to a stop in terms of his instincts and feelings. In fact, you could even argue that the opposite is true. I must say that, except for my time in the Ghetto—that is, most of the war—I didn't lack food or reasonably hygienic conditions, nor did my health suffer. First I lived the "good life" in Klwów with the peasant. As a cowherd, I wallowed all day long, watching the herd and, at harvest time, eating my fill of bread and drinking fresh milk to my heart's content.

In my first days on the Aryan side, I came to the house of a girl who was a bit older than me. I was an innocent lad, a "virgin." Back in school, my more experienced classmates used to tease me. If it had not been for that girl, who knows when I would have lost my virginity. She took care of my "education," telling me, "You must be in great distress and you need this badly." Then she gave me "lessons."

In the apartment at Panska 5, I met Irena Gelblum, who was called Irka. She won my heart. Marysia (Luba Gewisser) was Jurek's girl and Irena was mine. I loved Irena with all the fire of my youth, and we spent every free minute together. She was a beautiful girl with dreamy green eyes; she was very clever and intelligent and had a poetic soul. Irena performed the most dangerous errands. Antek assigned her to deliver weapons to Poniatów and Trawniki, which she did faithfully and with unusual success. Our love was subordinate to the conditions of the underground, the crowded apartment. But there was a public park in Warsaw and other places. We spent the whole war together. Perhaps our behavior didn't always please the "mothers and fathers of the movement" with whom we lived, or suit their notions of sexual purity. I must admit that they really were different from us and practiced what they preached and believed. Each of us in the underground lived in his own way under the Nazi occupation.

The "Black" Traitor

One of the people with whom I had contact with was a Pole, Stefan Pokropek. He would come regularly to the apartment at Waszingtona Boulevard 80, in Praga (the quarter east of the Wisla River). I also knew his daughter, who was my age. As we talked, I became interested in possible sources of weapons. At that time I was involved in acquiring weapons for our companions in Koniecpol, near Czestochowa, and in Czestochowa itself. In July or August 1943 Stefan invited me to his apartment to meet someone who, he said, "can help you in this matter." The man's name was "Black" (Czarny).

I had met Black about a month and a half before, on one of my visits to Stefan. He had showed up with a recommendation from a good friend of Stefan's, asking to join the partisans. Stefan himself didn't have any contacts, but I did, so he asked me to help the fellow join the "partisan ranks." A day or two later I talked to Antek about Black's request. Antek told the command staff of the AL, emphasizing that "since we don't know the man well, we aren't recommending him." A few days later the command staff told us that, after an investigation, they had decided to accept the man and take him into the underground in the city to carry out operations. But, at least for now, they wouldn't send him to a partisan unit in the forest.

A few weeks later, I was waiting for Black in a back room in Stefan's apartment, as we had agreed. He came on time and said he could provide us with a considerable quantity of bullets and weapons. He wanted to know if I had brought money for the deal. I said yes, and explained that he had to be very careful because such deals could easily result in complications or entrapment. Meanwhile, by sheer chance, Tadek Shayngut dropped in and joined the conversation. We agreed that Black would come back in an hour, bringing the weapons and ammunition, and we promised to give him the money on the spot. I asked Tadek to leave because anyone who wasn't vital to the operation shouldn't have been there. For some reason Tadek lingered; apparently he was curious, since such things didn't happen every day. Finally he gave in and left. But before he could get very far, we heard knocking and shouts of "Open up! Gestapo!" Stefan hurried to open the door. I asked him to wait a minute since there were already some weapons stockpiled in the apartment to be sent to the Czestochowa Ghetto; we had been interrupted while stripping, cleaning, assembling, and packing them. Aside from my revolver, we didn't have a single weapon ready to use. We behaved like inexperienced children.

Stefan's daughter, who was with us in the room, jumped out the window and I went after her. German bullets whizzed past my ears. I turned around once or twice to gauge the distance between me and the Gestapo agents, and saw that it was growing. Knowing the area well, I turned into a building that had a passage to another street and managed to get away from them. When the Gestapo agents burst into Stefan's apartment, they also discovered a Jew who was hiding there. I never knew who he was or anything about him except that Stefan, that good man, was hiding another Jew. That fellow was taken to the Gestapo station and tortured horribly. We later learned that he broke down under torture and "sang." Apparently he was the one who told the Gestapo about our other apartment, where Sara Biderman (Krysia) was hiding.

Stefan paid with his life for his faith in Black: the Germans killed him on the spot. The members of the AL who told us about it wept bitter tears for him. The man was loyal and devoted, both to them and to us.

After escaping from the house, I walked around the alleys until I was sure that contact was broken between me and the pursuers and that no one was tailing me. Then I slipped carefully into our apartment at Komitetowa Street 4 and told Antek what had happened. What worried us was that we were in the hands of a traitor who would denounce us. Theoretically, the whole thing might have been simple chance. Nevertheless, Antek and I were tormented by suspicion and, naturally, it focused on Black, who had recently joined the AL operations. Antek discussed his suspicions with the commanders of the AL, arguing that Black's credentials were hazy and not sufficiently reliable.

A week later, on a Sunday morning, I was innocently walking along Wolska Street, looking around as usual. I saw an open convertible, the kind the Germans used, approaching me. I recognized Black in it, sitting next to uniformed Gestapo agents. He noticed me and, as the car drove by, started shouting, "Halt! Hands up! Halt!" He called out a mixture of German and Polish curses, and I went on walking as if the cries weren't aimed at me. At that hour the street was teeming with people going to church or coming back. I continued walking at a normal pace and suddenly swooped into the crowd, mingled with the people, and disappeared from Black's view. Once again I had escaped. At any rate, it was now absolutely clear that he was the reason Tadek and the anonymous Jew had been killed and the weapons for Czestochowa had been confiscated. I immediately reported the traitor to the AL. The incident was one of our major failures.

Before that personal meeting with Black on Wolska Street, I happened on a Gypsy woman on some street (close to Komitetowa Street 4). She pleaded with me and promised to tell me interesting things; I gave in. We went inside the gate of one of the buildings and she started telling my future from her cards. "The gentleman is in great danger," she said. "Death is lurking on every side." Among other things, she mentioned Krysia and said I would hear from her in a few days. I burst out laughing, since the only Krysia I knew had been caught and shot. A crowd of onlookers had gathered around us. I paid the Gypsy woman and went on my way.

Back in the apartment I told Antek, Zivia, and Marek the story. We all laughed uproariously. They made fun of me for listening to a Gypsy woman's tales—which was dangerous as well as laughable (since Gentiles had gathered around).

Then came miracles and surprises. A few days later we received instructions to contact Dr. Bilecki.[63] We were told that he would give us information about Krysia. We hesitated in case it was a trap, but eventually decided to check him out. One day I set out for the Bilecki home. I identified myself to Hela, Dr. Bilecki's daughter, who told me that Krysia really was there. I was stunned and suspected another trap. But Hela looked and spoke sincerely and seemed to be telling the truth. She said the Germans had dragged Krysia to a grove near the place where she had been hiding. They had shot her and left her for dead. After lying like that for at least ten hours, Krysia had collected what little strength she had left and had managed to reach the Bilecki home. Apparently, it was the only address she could remember. Hela, who had been Krysia's classmate, immediately saw how serious her condition was and took her to the hospital, where part of her intestine was removed. Ultimately, Krysia recovered, thanks to a physician who was one of Dr. Bilecki's friends. After a brief convalescence in the hospital, Krysia was moved to the apartment of the Bileckis, who were active members of the underground. For Krysia's own good, they thought it was better for her not to stay with them.

I promised Hela to remove Krysia as soon as possible. I consulted with Antek and Zivia, and we decided to bring her to Panska 5. It wasn't terribly smart to concentrate so many people in one place, but we had no choice. I contacted Hela,

63. Dr. Bilecki, a Polish engineer, was deputy minister of transportation in Poland after the war. According to Zuckerman (1993: 437), he was imprisoned in Auschwitz because of this incident. He died a few years after the war.

we made the proper arrangements, and Krysia was brought to our apartment.

The Apartment at Wolska Street 6

Wolska Street was in a typical Polish Christian neighborhood inhabited mostly by working-class Poles. We had concluded that it would be wise for our people to live in several apartments. It was important for Antek to live separately, to minimize the risk of exposure. As soon as he came out of the Ghetto, he moved into an apartment that we obtained with the help of the AL underground. I should point out that our contacts with the AL were through Jewish friends who for some reason chose to work in the Scouts movement. I've already said that Luba rented the apartment at Panska 5 through the connections of her friend Jurek, who was a member of the Scouts, and those same contacts helped get us the apartment at Wolska 6. It belonged to the wife of a Polish officer who was a prisoner of war in Germany. She lived alone and was told that Antek was a Jew, while I was introduced as a Christian, a member of the Polish underground who would live with him "for underground work." And we did operate from that apartment. We left every morning at 7:30 or 8, on foot. To avoid surprises, we didn't use the tram or any other public transportation, since the Germans tended to stop and search those vehicles suddenly. When you go by foot, you can look far ahead, and if something is going on, you can retreat. We would walk five or six kilometers to the center of the city and separate, each of us off to his own business. As curfew approached, we would meet to return to the apartment together.

In the center of the city, you didn't stand out because of the density of the population. It was hard to identify you even if you came back to the meeting place several times. Incidentally, the members of the Polish underground we met with would always fix the place.

One evening as I returned home, the landlady asked me, "Are you really a Pole? I think you're also a Jew." She looked at me obliquely. I burst out laughing and replied on the spot, "I'm willing to prove it to you, madam." She said, "Please, sir, prove it!" I unbuckled my belt, unbuttoned my fly, and pulled down my pants; when I was down to my underwear, she turned around and walked out. This was the kind of "existential problem" you came across on a normal day; it was not unique at all.

We shared the bathroom in the apartment but took care of our own food, laundry, and such. This was in December 1943 and January 1944. The temperature outside was below zero—freezing cold. In the morning we ate little cubes of lard washed down with vodka. We got the lard from Kajszczak, the peasant from the village of Lomianki; we stayed in touch with him even after our comrades were removed from the forest near his village. Food in the city was rationed, so we mostly used the black market. Pork could be found only on the black market that flourished in the Aryan district. Dealing on the black market was a crime, but it didn't involve mortal danger. On the other hand, smuggling weapons or possessing an underground newspaper really was dangerous.

We had scant means and were careful to make do with little. We ate only one meal a day.

From Wolska 6 we stayed in touch with the other apartments and sometimes even ate there. Sometimes we made ourselves a meal. One thing we consumed without limit and didn't skimp on was cigarettes. We spent most of our daily budget on cigarettes, which could be bought in kiosks. You could buy two or three individual cigarettes, not necessarily a full pack, even before the war, not to mention in wartime. We generally smoked Wanda cigarettes, a cheap brand. Sometimes we managed to get German cigarettes smuggled into the black market by soldiers. These were flat and very tasty.

It is hard for me to remember why we left the apartment

on Wolska Street. At a certain stage we started organizing a central apartment for the members of the ZOB in Warsaw. We got hold of an apartment—in the name of Marysia Sawicka—at Leszno Street 18, an area that had once been inside the Ghetto, in a house next to a church. During the Ghetto days, I used to see converted Jews going to pray in the church. We built a hiding place in the apartment with a double wall; we "stole" a section of the room and carefully disguised the entrance to the hideout.

In 1944 that apartment was inhabited by Zivia, Antek, Marek Edelman, me, Leyzer Levin and his son, Stefan Grajek, Krysia, Tuvia Borzykowski, and Yosef Sak.[64]

Now and then, Antek would send me to certain places in the city to hear the news on the BBC or from Moscow, and I would come back and report to him. We didn't have a single radio in the ZOB, not even in our apartment-bases. We didn't want to take the risk, since listening to foreign stations was strictly prohibited. Possessing a receiving and transmitting instrument was not even to be mentioned. Antek always knew what was going on around him and in the world. Even in times of weakness, as when the Ghetto Uprising was being crushed or when we learned of the suicide of Franya Beatus,

---

64. Leyzer Levin was one of the organizers of Po'alei Zion Z.S. in the underground. He was active in the Jewish Self-Help Society (YISA), supervised soup kitchens in the Ghetto, and escaped to the Aryan side during the April Uprising. He died in Israel in 1967, at age 76. Stefan Grajek, born in Warsaw, was one of the founders of the Po'alei Zion Z.S. underground in Warsaw. He too escaped to the Aryan side after the April Uprising. Later he fought in the Polish Uprising and participated in Brikha. He immigrated to Israel. Joseph Sak, born in Przemysl, taught literature in Czestochowa. A social activist in the Warsaw Ghetto, he was one of the founders and directors of the Dror underground gymnasium and a member of the Anti-Fascist Bloc. He died in Israel in 1965, at age 67.

his curiosity and awareness never flagged. I went to listen as ordered, and I returned and reported.

I have absolutely no memory of the people or the code words that got me into the hiding place/apartment to hear what I heard. But I am sure that, at least a few times, I visited the apartments of AK and AL members to listen to the radio broadcasts. I vaguely remember a field, on the edges of the forest, at night; torches are lit and people are waiting for a parachutist or a few parachutists, who were to land from British airplanes—couriers of the Government-in-Exile in London. I was there to get or do something, but I can't give details. It had something to do with the Yakov Wernik case.

Yakov Wernik was one of the few who were rescued from Treblinka. He ran away during the uprising that erupted there in August 1943. We got word that "a Jew had escaped from Treblinka," and I was sent to see him and hear what he had to say. He was staying in a dark chamber, where I sat with him and listened to his story. He described vividly what had happened at Treblinka; he sounded authentic, honest, warm. At Zivia's and Antek's request, his words were written down, and that was the first report transmitted to London and published there and in America. It was Wernik who built the model of Treblinka at the museum in Lohamei Ha-Gettaot. When I met him then, on the outskirts of Warsaw, I promised to stay in touch with him, and said he could count on our help. Only then did he start telling his tale. I was impressed with his "good"—that is, Aryan—looks, and I even told Antek that I thought the man could move around freely and disguise himself as a Christian.

On a Mission to Wyszków Forest

We made contact with a group of companions who had survived the Ghetto Uprising and had been moved from Lomianki Forest to Wyszków Forest. It was decided that I should visit them. The date and time were set in advance, and one of them was to wait for me at the train station near the forest. On the appointed day I went with a Bundist, Celeminski, to Wyszków. We got off at the station. There was no signpost, and we didn't know which way to go. Our friends had agreed to wait nearby, at the edge of the forest. We asked one of the station workers to show us the way. As soon as we mentioned the name of the place, I sensed that we drew attention. As we left in the direction indicated to us by the station worker, I turned my head and saw that we were being followed. At the edge of the forest, we met Jakobek (Yakov Putermilch) and another friend, Janek Bielak. After a joyful greeting, we started walking toward the hiding place of the ZOB group. On the way we met a peasant who warned us that the Germans were searching the forest. Our companions, who were experienced partisans, ignored the warning and said, "It's not so. We were just there. They just want to scare us."

I didn't want to look like a coward, but I did advise them to be careful; the peasant may have been telling the truth. They laughed at me.

The weather was beautiful. The forest smelled nice. We were in a good mood. We joked and told stories. I had a camera with me, and on the way I photographed my friends. At some distance from the base, the two gave the agreed-on whistle and listened for the answer indicating all was well. But no answer whistled back in the forest. We started crawling toward the fighters' base. When we got close enough to see what was going on, we realized no one was there. We came closer. From the condition of the objects on the ground and the smoke still rising from the bonfire, we concluded that our friends had fled in panic. I photographed the deserted camp from various angles. Shoes, clothes, and various other objects had been left helter-skelter. We also got out in a hurry. Clearly, the peasant's warning had been true. Not that we deserved praise for our wisdom; it was only our luck that saved us. If we had gotten there a little bit earlier, we would have fallen in the trap.

We went on a bit and found a hiding place where, following the advice of our two companions, we stayed until dark. When night fell, we returned to the base to check whether any of our friends had returned. Again the whistle was sounded, again we waited. To our surprise, this time an answer came. In a partially destroyed encampment, we met the members of the group, who said that the Germans had come, searched the forest, and, amazingly, failed to discover them. When we arrived, the Germans were still nearby, so they didn't want to answer the whistle. We stayed there overnight. Our companions at the base celebrated our visit with a special treat—potato dumplings with flour, a dish they cooked in a bucket. When they had finished their work, they invited us to eat. So we fished dumplings out of the bucket and ate them, all together.

The next day, before returning to Warsaw, we faced a serious problem: when we got up in the morning, we found ourselves swarming with lice. We couldn't take the train back to Warsaw in that condition, since we might look suspicious. A few friends decided to take care of each of us and gave us a thorough delousing.

I took several more photos of all corners of the base; I also photographed our friends individually and in groups. We parted warmly, and I promised to come visit them again soon. Naturally, such photos couldn't be given to just anyone to develop. My Bundist friend claimed he had a photographer who could be trusted. So I gave the film to Celeminski—and never saw either the film or a picture again. My repeated requests in the years since have been in vain. I even offered him a deal—I'd get one copy of every photo and would give up the negatives—but I didn't get a single picture. I knew the pictures weren't excellent as professional photography, but I thought they had historical value. It's hard for me to remember where I got hold of the camera, but it is clear to me that I took it with me on purpose. After the war, some of these pictures were published in various books.

While we're on the subject of photographs, in a few places a photo was published showing Antek walking on a Warsaw street, in May 1943, with Tadek Siewierski and me walking in front of him like bodyguards. This is how that picture came to be taken: We were walking down the street and a street-photographer approached us. I signaled to him, "Shoot!" In spite of the danger, I wanted to be photographed, perhaps out of mischief. I got a note from the photographer and, a few days later, I went and picked up the picture. My friends were mad at me: "You're careless, you don't know who the photographer is." I told them he photographed a lot of people in the street and it wasn't so bad. All the photographs were lost, except one that remained with Marysia Sawicka. This is the only authentic photo we have left from that period.

I visited our friends in Wyszków Forest several times, always raising the question, Which was smarter and safer: to go on hiding in the forest or to move to one of the houses prepared for them in Warsaw? Every one of them wanted to discuss that privately with me. Not a single one tried to make a deal with me to take him out. They wanted to talk privately because it was more comfortable to unburden themselves that way. I had several conversations like that with our companions. I had to mobilize all my emotional force not to explode. I was uncomfortable in this situation, since I was a "city boy," ostensibly living a good life and enjoying all the fruits of that world. It was hard for me to explain to them, to convey to them the sense of what it meant to live in the city in those days. They lived in the forest, under difficult conditions, without a house, without a bed or chairs, and there wasn't always food. It was very hard for me to advise them, and I was especially careful about words that might be misinterpreted. I felt that they envied me for living in the city, for not being a partisan in the forest.

Apparently I could afford to see the advantages and disadvantages of life in the forest—of being a partisan and fighting, on the one hand, and, on the other hand, of being in the city and living underground. Looking like a Christian, I was assigned to live and operate in the city, always with an assumed identity. If it had been up to me, I think I would have chosen to live in the forest. But I certainly couldn't tell them that, because I was afraid it would be misinterpreted. Hence, I tried to list the pros and cons, one against the other, and especially the dangers of each of the choices. I left the final decision up to them, and everyone decided as he liked. I am sure that, in the short run and in terms of comfort, city life was easier. On the other hand, life in the forest was a lot safer in the long run and provided greater chances of staying alive. In the forest, there was less direct and immediate danger. It may seem strange that, in a fighting organization like the ZOB, everyone could choose. We saw our struggle in the Ghetto as the essential purpose; afterward it was much more important to us to rescue, to "protect" the people, to save their lives, as much as possible.

On my second visit to the comrades in Wyszków, I didn't ask directions at the railroad station, since I knew the way. Our friends led me to the encampment without incident. This time, too, they wanted to have private conversations with me. The subject on the agenda again was whether to continue in the forest or to move to a hideout in Warsaw. Ultimately, some of them, including Jakobek and his wife, decided to move to the city. We did what they wanted.

During my stay in Wyszków, our friends decided to introduce me to a man who helped them, a forest ranger who lived deep in the forest. It was important for them to introduce me as a member of the Polish underground, as an insurance pol-

icy for them. We went a long way until we came to a hut in
the forest. On the way, it rained and we were soaked to the
skin, and the idea of being inside the hut, warming myself at
a fire, delighted me. They knocked on the door. After uttering
the password, we went in, sat down, and relaxed. We even
took off our wet shoes and socks and put them on the fire-
place to dry. No one was home except the grandmother, who
gave us hot tea and said that the man of the house would
come soon. There were about six or seven of us in the group.
As we sat there cozily, drinking tea and talking, we suddenly
heard a volley of shots. We leaped out of our chairs as if we
had been bitten by snakes. The shots increased. We thought
we had been discovered and that the house was surrounded.
We took up positions. I felt unbelievably bad: I was the only
one without a weapon, lying on the floor and waiting, with
thoughts running through my mind: Is this the end? The
shooting grew louder. One of us peeped outside and reported,
"Those aren't Germans, they're partisans shooting." "Is that
the anti-Semitic faction of the AK?" We told the old woman
that the men outside looked like peasants and that they were
shooting at us. The woman immediately grasped what was
happening and, as the shooting continued, she opened the
door and shouted in that direction, "Stop it, they're our people!" All at once, the shooting stopped.

Later, we learned that one of the family saw us go into the
hut, thought it was a rival partisan group, and called his
friends from the nearby village to attack us. After everything
was settled safely, we celebrated the happy ending with some
hot tea.

Our friends introduced me to the forest ranger. I played
the role of an underground member who had come "straight
from the center," which made an impression on the locals.
They were honored to entertain a city man, who was also an
"important" member of the underground.

I was assigned to meet representatives of the AK in the

Wyszków area to try to settle relations between the AK and
the ZOB in the forest. The ZOB group had called us in and
complained bitterly that the AK were conspiring against
them, and in fact wanted to destroy them. With Antek's in-
tervention, we got in touch with someone from headquarters who was in charge of the area. He gave us data and
details about holding a meeting with the AK underground
commander, who would settle relations between the two
sides. We wanted them to stop harming our fellows in the
forest. Accompanied by several armed companions, I went
to the meeting place. In honor of the event our friends wore
festive attire; miraculously, one of them had even miraculously gotten hold of a starched collar, cuffs, and tie. He
looked elegant and formal, even though he didn't have a
shirt on his back.

Our companions pleaded with me to be very careful at the
meeting. They said it wasn't inconceivable that the AK
would try to kill us either during the meeting or on our way
to it. We agreed that some of our companions would cover
us from a distance and, if need be, defend us. We arrived first
at the meeting, and a few moments later our partners showed
up. After a few polite words, I brought up the problem. To
reinforce what I said, I introduced myself as a member of the
AK in Warsaw, working on their behalf, which was only
partly correct, since I really was working "on their behalf"
but hadn't been appointed by them. In a conversation of
about half an hour, I explained that the AK command wanted
them to make peace with the ZOB, and I scolded them for
what they had done in the past. Apparently my mission succeeded since, before we parted, my interlocutors promised to
make every effort to ensure the safety of our people. In return,
they asked the members of the ZOB not to pester the peasants in the area. In fact, things did calm down in the area for
some time, which made our companions feel safer.

The meeting is described in one of Antek's letters

from that period, now in the archive at Beit Lohamei Ha-Gettaot:[65]

> Yesterday, Kazik came back from the forest. It's lucky he went. He met there with the representatives of the 'Sikorskys' [the AK]. The situation is portrayed like this: The intelligence (of the AK) denounces them as a gang condemned to destruction. The representative tells him (Kazik) that they want to check who this gang belongs to; if it's the PZP, they would leave them alone.[66] The representative (of the AK) himself says that the gang doesn't support itself by robbing. (On the other hand) the PPR treats our group as 'its own people,' who have a certain autonomy. Recently, they carried out an armed attack in cooperation (with us). The PPR thinks the group is acting correctly (they know about their contacts with AK) otherwise (if it's the AK), they would have destroyed them. The pair agrees to meet with Commander Wolomon on Monday, instead of Kazik. A letter according to which the group belongs to the PZP. I sent for Waclaw today and told him of the situation. I'm waiting for his answer on this.

In this period of my operations, there were other kinds of acts, which I tell not as gossip but as reality, pure and simple.

One day we got word that one of the girls in the Wyszków group was pregnant and had to have an abortion. Clearly, under the conditions in the forest, in 1943, with no foreseeable end to the war, female fighters couldn't allow themselves to

65. Lohamei Ha-Gettaot, the Ghetto Fighters' Kibbutz in Israel, has an important museum and an extensive archive on the Holocaust.

66. The PZP (Polski Zwiazek Powstanczy) was the Polish Insurgents' Union.

have babies. One of our members, a physician by profession, agreed to perform the abortion, but he needed instruments. He gave us a detailed list, and we made monumental efforts to get the necessary instruments and send them to the forest as soon as possible. With the help of Polish friends and acquaintances, including doctors, we managed to get hold of or buy the instruments, in drugstores and various shops, and sent them to the forest. One night, in the forest, by candlelight, in one of the trenches, the operation was performed. Several months later the woman gave birth to a baby: the abortion hadn't been done properly and the fetus hadn't been destroyed. Our people were afraid that the fetus would be maimed. The baby's father, Gavrish Fryszdorf, was killed in an operation in the forest before his baby was born. The woman, Hanka (née Zucker), was brought to Warsaw in the seventh month of her pregnancy and gave birth during the Polish Uprising to a hale and healthy baby. Mother and baby both survived.[67]

The last contact we had with our companions in Wyszków was a week before the Polish Uprising. We sent couriers to bring Pnina Papier and Haim Grinshpan to Warsaw, taking clothes to make it easier for them to move to the city. Dov Shniper, the commander of their partisan group, decided he would go with Pnina and ordered Haim to stay in the forest. Haim's explanations that Kazik's written instructions were for the couriers to bring both Pnina and Haim were all in vain. Dov was killed in Warsaw in the early days of the Polish Uprising in 1944. When he was discovered by the Germans, he opened fire on them and was shot to death. Janek Bielak, who was also brought to Warsaw just before

67. Gabriel (Gavrish) and Hannah (Hanka) Fryszdorf, veteran Bundists and ZOB members, fought in the April Uprising. Hannah Fryszdorf worked at the YIVO Jewish Research Institute in New York until her death in 1989.

the outbreak of the Polish Uprising, was killed along with Dov.

Finding a Hideout

A considerable part of our work was devoted to taking care of our people: finding hiding places—either in the city and its suburbs, or in other cities, especially after the Polish Uprising; and moving people, most of whom didn't have documents, from place to place. I learned that a person in the underground unwittingly adopts the responses of a pursued person, and thus may be an easy prey to every passer-by, not to mention Gestapo agents. The Germans' internal security system was extensive and varied, and was assisted by local residents. Just as there were many Poles—especially underground members—who gave us a hand, there were also many others who hunted Jews to do a "good deed," sometimes even gratis. One of the tricks we used to increase the safety of Jews in hiding was to hint to the Polish landlords that we were working for the underground—either the AK or the AL, depending on the landlord's affinities.

We never introduced ourselves explicitly as underground members; it was hinted at in various ways, and we were helped—not always wittingly—by our contacts in the underground. Such visits cheered our companions in their hideouts and relieved their harsh isolation, but they were also aimed at the rescuers. In general, when a Polish Christian who gave protection to a Jew learned that a Polish underground group was also interested in the fate of those hiding, and even came to visit them, the Jew's stock rose in their eyes. The Pole was also filled with the sense that his activity was important and necessary and that, somewhere, he was registered in the "annals of the underground." Clearly, every visit was a blessing, but every visit was also liable to bring disaster. We had to be extremely careful, and when approaching the hideout, we had to be absolutely sure we weren't being followed. We were already experienced in this.

In time, a routine of visits was created: everyone had a group "under his protection," meaning that he had to make sure that all the costs of maintenance reached the group and their landlords. Every courier had dozens of people in his charge whom he had to visit and take care of. Money was one of the most important things, but it wasn't the only one. In general, we made sure that every Jew in hiding had forged papers in case of emergency. We also took care of bringing news from underground publications to encourage and cheer them up. Naturally, people had different personal needs, and sometimes we had to supply medicine and doctors. This gave us a lot of trouble because, except for Inka, there weren't any physicians among us. We relied on outside doctors who were willing to help us.

We didn't make contact too frequently for two reasons. First, the number of our couriers was small enough to be counted on the fingers of both hands. The second reason involved the risk that the hideout would be discovered. As a rule, every house in Warsaw had a concierge who gave information to the police on everything that went on in the house and reported on tenants and visitors, not to mention strangers. The concierges would investigate strangers to find out which of the tenants the stranger was visiting and why.

You had to stay away from the concierges, but that wasn't easy. They had a hand in exposing and destroying many Jews. Therefore, we avoided frequent visits. We didn't keep lists of people and addresses. I contrived a system for myself for finding streets and people, and to this day I can't get away from it. I always identified the house and the precise place I was in without knowing the name of the street or the number of the house. This was done with the idea that, if we were caught and interrogated, they wouldn't get details that could harm our friends. What we didn't know we couldn't reveal to others.

Whenever possible, we introduced ourselves as members of the Polish underground, as "proper Christians." Even someone who was involved in underground work couldn't call us liars, since there was a special department in the AK named the Committee to Aid Jews (Rada Pomocy Zydom). Aside from maintaining contact with people in and around Warsaw, we also stayed in touch with Jews in other cities and with our companions in various places in the General-gouvernement. I personally took care of such issues in several places, like Lomianki Forest and then Wyszków Forest, Cze-stochowa, Koniecpol, Krakow, Plaszów, Trawniki, Poniatów, and Skarzysko. I was really "at home" on the Otwock line (the railroad line to spas south of the capital).

Money to support the Jews in hiding came to us through the Polish underground, which was connected with the Po-lish Government-in-Exile in London. The money came to Warsaw and all foreign currency was changed into local money at the unofficial rate. Antek took care of that. He of-ten told of his arguments with members of the Polish under-ground about the exchange rate, because the money was transferred from abroad in dollars, Swiss francs, and even gold bullion.[68] The money came from the Jewish Agency, the Joint, and special Bundist sources.[69] I understood from the

68. Antek told of his problems with the Polish underground: "For weeks, they would hold onto the money sent to us from London. Not to mention how they cheated us by getting the money in pounds sterling or dollars, selling it on the black market, and giving us only a small fraction in dollars or sterling; they would give us the rest according to the official German rate, which was perhaps 10 percent of the black market rate. Thus they discounted the sums sent for us a great deal" (Zuckerman 1993: 419).

69. The Jewish Agency was the international Zionist government before the state of Israel. The Joint (American Jewish Joint Distri-

conversations among the "bigwigs" that we didn't get all the money sent to us from the United States, Britain, and Switzerland. On the way part of it was "swallowed" by couriers and various members of the underground. I can testify only that a lot of money did arrive, at least after June 1943.

We set ourselves a monthly budget, which was spent on the most necessary items. When I was out of the house, the money was enough for cigarettes, trips, and one meal a day. We always tried to be together in a group, insofar as possible, for security reasons. Zivia took charge of the budget: she ran the house, decided what would be bought, and fixed the daily menu. She was the sole authority in this area and had the last word.

To Zivia I was always Kaziutka, to others only sometimes. She gave me this nickname to show her special feelings for me. Despite our verbal confrontation during the exodus from the sewers, we felt sincere friendship and mutual appreciation for one another. I knew that Zivia—or, as we called her then, by her underground name, Celina—had absolute trust in me, which was sometimes hard for me. We got along extraordinarily well, and I can't remember a single argument about how we performed our underground work. She took care of all my needs as only a "Jewish mother" can.

The only luxury on the menu was a glass of vodka—and we insisted firmly on that. Clothing was also analyzed according to the most vital needs. Those like me, who walked around outside a lot—and we tried as much as possible not to use public transportation—needed warm clothes in winter, whereas those in hiding needed practically no new clothes.

---

bution Committee) was founded in 1914 as the Joint Distribution Committee of American Funds for the Relief of Jewish War Sufferers. Between 1939 and 1945 it spent almost eighty million dollars for relief and rescue of Jews in Europe.

One of the people I came in contact with as a courier was Adolf Berman, called "Adam."[70] He lived most of the time with his wife, Batya (Basha), and they moved from place to place together. I used to bring him letters from Antek, including Yiddish ones, with information and activity reports. Among other things, Adam was also the archivist of the Jewish National Committee.[71] Adam, Antek, and another member constituted its presidium. In underground conditions, the battles and the moving around, Adam managed to rescue and preserve everything that might have any historical value: strips of paper, copies of reports, publications, propaganda leaflets, and so forth. In time, he amassed an important archive, which is now at Beit Lohamei Ha-Gettaot. Recently, I glanced at some notes and letters in Antek's handwriting from 1943 and 1944; some of them say that I am to take a message or bring an answer to Antek. I must admit that, unfortunately, the notes, which are 100 percent authentic, do not jog my memory or remind me of where I took them from or brought them to. In her book *Underground Diary*, Batya Berman devotes a special chapter to Irka and me, describing our activity as couriers; there I am the "shadow" of Irka, who brought them messages and other material.[72] Batya even de-

70. Adolf Berman (1906–), born in Warsaw, was a member of Po'alei Zion Left, director of CENTOS (Centrala Opieki nad Sierotami, or Organization for the Care of Orphans) and active in the underground. He coedited the Anti-Fascist Bloc newspaper - *Der Ruf*. In the summer of 1942 he went to the Aryan side of Warsaw, where he fought in the Polish Uprising. After the Liberation, until late 1946, he was a member of the Polish Provisional Government. He immigrated to Israel in 1950.

71. The political arm of the ZOB.

72. *Underground Diary* was published in Hebrew by Beit Lohamei Hagettaot (Tel Aviv, 1956).

scribes how we quarreled with her. I swear I remember only good things about Batya Berman. I remember that, after I came back from a visit to Koniecpol and Czestochowa, in May 1944, a mission I accomplished with the Polish policeman Adamczyk, I brought "mail" to Adam from his friends trapped in HASAG Czestochowa.

I also visited the hiding place of Jakobek and Masha (Yakov and Masha Putermilch), who had been brought to the city from the Wyszków Forest. Twice I went with Antek to visit them. The couple greeted us nicely and took pains to make us treats to "refresh the soul," but also to show the landlords that they were visited by important members of the underground. Apparently, Antek was in a good mood. He sat down and started telling stories, as he had done in the past; unfortunately, I only rarely got to hear them.

I should tell a few details—even if not in chronological order—about some of the dangers we faced when we were forced to move our comrades from one hiding place to another.

About a week after the comrades came out of the manhole on Prosta Street, on May 17, 1943, Antek, Marek Folman, and I went to visit them in Lomianki Forest.[73] Tuvia Borzykowski was very sick and had to be taken to Warsaw. We knew that riding the tram was very dangerous. First of all, you encountered a group of people whose eyes were incessantly questioning and examining you. And I must say they had a sharp and discerning eye for Jews, even from a distance.

---

73. Marek Folman, born in Miechów, was active in Dror and one of the founders of the Dror underground gymnasium in the Warsaw Ghetto. Caught by the Nazis in the January Uprising in 1943, he was sent to Treblinka but escaped and returned to Warsaw. With the ZOB on the Aryan side, he participated in the April Uprising. He was shot and killed in the railroad station in Czestochowa at age 27.

Tuvia, who had a very high fever, certainly would have attracted attention. His clothes weren't in such good shape either, since he had been out of the Ghetto only a week, and his frightened eyes and movements seemed to invite suspicion. We decided, therefore, to make our way on foot. It was far—twelve to fifteen kilometers. We set out, Antek and Tuvia leading the way, Marek and I bringing up the rear. The two of us pretended to be jolly, walking and carrying on a loud conversation, all the while looking around. It was a beautiful, sunny spring day, the trees were in bloom, the street was bustling with pedestrians, including Germans—some rushing off to their business, others strolling leisurely.

For Tuvia, this was a completely different world from what he had been used to for all those months in the Ghetto. The way his back twitched showed how moved he was by the experience. The closer we came to the city, the greater was the danger of discovery. I didn't know if he had enough emotional strength to overcome his physical exhaustion and high fever. We went on our way, pretending everything was just fine. Marek Folman and I tried to distract ourselves from the imminent danger with our loud conversation. We both realized that if our two comrades walking ahead were stopped, we would have to act immediately. We were armed with pistols. I knew Marek well. He was a wonderful fellow and we had quickly become friends. I felt that he could be trusted in time of trouble.

After this forced march of almost four hours (given Tuvia's condition), we reached our destination at Komitetowa Street 4. We had selected that place as a residence for Tuvia for the foreseeable future. As we approached the house, Antek and Tuvia were swallowed up in the gate—a sign to Marek and me that our job was finished. Tuvia joined the inhabitants of the hideout behind the bookshelf and stayed in the apartment until the incident of blackmail I described before.

Of Apartments and People

Felek Rajszczak, a Pole, a first-rate builder, a dedicated Communist from his youth, was a man you trusted from the first moment.[74] Felek was a friend of Stefan (Grajek), and one day he was asked to build a hideout in an apartment we had acquired for that purpose on Twarda Street. Felek and his family were supposed to live there as tenants. After renovations, the family—which included his wife Veronica, his daughter Mirka, and his son Tadek—moved into the apartment. It was a big flat where a brick wall was built in the end room, reducing the room by about two feet; in the wall, a big heating oven covered with white tiles, as was common then, was built. The heating compartment in the bottom half of the oven, surrounded by a special iron frame set in a track, served as a passage between the two parts of the room. The passage was very uncomfortable, but the camouflage was perfect. Felek held onto his former apartment, even though most of the time the entire family lived in the new apartment and were accepted by the tenants of the building. Felek was an experienced member of the underground and knew he couldn't reveal his activity to his children. I introduced myself as a Pole, a member of the underground, maintaining contact with the Jews hiding in their house.

The family went on with their normal life. Relatives, friends, and acquaintances came to visit, and neighbors also

74. Rajszczak was a steadfast friend of the Jews, which resulted in his capture by the German criminal police (Kripo). On Feb. 19, 1944, Antek wrote to one of his colleagues in an attempt to find some way to get him out of that predicament: "We got a letter today from Grajek's landlord from the *Kripo*; they beat him hard to make him turn over Antek and Kazik. The landlord claims he doesn't know any Antek and that he saw Kazik only once. He asks us to rescue him. . . . His name is Felix Rajszczak (born in 1901)" (Zuckerman 1993: 491).

dropped in sometimes. As usual, the Rajszczak family was instructed in all the rules of caution. They always had to stall before opening the door to unexpected visitors, to invent plausible excuses, in order to allow our companions enough time to crawl into the hiding place. Leyzer Levin and his son, Yosef Sak, Tuvia Borzykowski, and Stefan Grajek stayed in that apartment for a certain time. I would regularly visit our friends on Sundays and, if need be, during the week as well. I normally ate lunch with the Rajszczak family every Sunday. Once Felek turned to me during lunch and said, "Kazik, why aren't you eating? Eat something, please." "I'm eating, Felek," I answered. He replied, "Kazik, I asked you to eat and you gorge yourself, bastard." On these occasions Mirka, who was two years younger than me, would bake cakes they were forbidden to taste until I came. The family, and especially the father, would joke that she kept the cake just for me. Mirka's relations to me, surrounded as I was by the halo of the underground, created a very awkward situation. Even during the war, young people normally went out. Mirka didn't know I was a Jew, and I had to find some excuse for not wanting to go out. Once I gave in to her request, to avoid doubts about my being a Pole, and we went to the movies.

Tadek, the son, was devoted and did any little errand I asked him. He helped me from time to time, since, as a boy—he was about fourteen—nobody would suspect him.

But that apartment was also discovered. We were forced to leave it after the landlord was caught by the Gestapo. In fact, the man was caught because of us: we got word that Jews were still hiding in the Ghetto and organized an operation to rescue them. A few people were brought out and taken to a hiding place prepared in advance. One day I asked Felek to accompany me as a builder and to suggest a plan for a hideout. There he met the son of the landlord of the apartment we wanted to turn into a hiding place. The son may have been the spy, since he was later revealed as a Gestapo agent—such things often happened. As a result, Felek was arrested on January 11, 1944, and was interrogated at length and repeatedly. They were most interested in learning where Antek and Kazik were hiding. (Antek had been with me in the apartment at least once or twice, and his name may have been mentioned by the informer.) Felek told me the story after he was released by the Gestapo: at a certain stage of the interrogation and torture, he was asked if he knew we were Jews; he answered that he didn't know Antek and Kazik were Jews. Now that he knew, he added, he had no more reason to hide them, but he simply didn't know where they were. Apparently, that was a convincing argument; the fact is, Felek was released.

We also did all we could (with the help of various couriers), including bribing Gestapo agents, to free Felek. Obviously, the Gestapo was working sloppily here too, since, a couple of days after he was arrested and not knowing anything about it, I returned to the apartment to get details about the plan for the hideout—and they didn't catch me.

In the Gestapo, Felek had been confronted with Natek, who had been captured under other circumstances but was also involved in the rescue operation and in the preparation of the hideout. He too had been subjected to severe torture and interrogation. As far as we knew, Natek had broken one day and, as a result (although it is not known for sure), a few of the apartment hiding places had been discovered. Natek also knew the apartment on Panska Street, Luba and Irena's apartment, but he hadn't revealed that. We learned then that, being unable to bear the torture of the interrogation, he had "volunteered" to lead the Gestapo to a made-up place; once outside the Gestapo building, he had begun running away but was shot by the Germans and killed.

I must add a few words about Natek. I used him from mid-1943, after Luba's Jurek recommended him to Antek as a "fellow you could trust, inventive, loyal, clever." Antek suggested I get him into underground work on the Aryan side, and I did. Natek didn't work with us for long because he was captured. I still remember him. He was a fine fellow. As for the rest—who can judge a person who endured the tortures of the Gestapo for weeks?

I was deeply concerned about Felek, who endangered his whole family to help us. After he was released by the Gestapo, I had an argument with my friends. They all thought we should stay away from Felek. In terms of underground logic, Zivia, Antek, Marek, and the others were right; but I felt we owed him a lot and had to meet him, even if it was dangerous. I decided to go to him and didn't hide it from my friends. One evening I reconnoitered near his house. I realized (with relative certainty) that there was no observation or search around the apartment, and I went in. Felek was very glad to see me. Although he was much older than me, we were fond of each other. He told me of the interrogations and tortures he had undergone and about his meeting with Natek, when Natek had told the Germans he knew Felek. Felek said, "I denied it, I kept denying we knew each other." Felek was a powerful man who had become a broken vessel, but I must emphasize that he remained firm despite everything he had been through and said he was willing to go on working with us.

Felek slowly recovered his strength and we decided to use him again in a special job—planning a serious hideout, which would be the base of our operations, in one of the houses we had acquired in the Bernerowo neighborhood, in a Warsaw suburb. We thought we needed this house because a lot of apartments had been discovered when Natek and Felek had been arrested. I mention this only in terms of the calendar, without intending to imply a clear connection between their arrest and the discovery of the apartments.

There were several large rooms in this building, and a hiding place built there could accommodate a large number of people, if necessary. It took several months to build this hideout because we couldn't use strangers to work on it, and everything was done by Felek. Sometimes he was assisted by his young son, Tadek; and when I had time from my work, I also would help finish the construction. Once, when I was busy working with Felek, an accident happened that could have cost us dear: we were doing something in a gigantic concrete pipe when the pipe suddenly collapsed. Miraculously, we got out safe and sound.

One day when I went with Felek to buy some building materials, we were stopped by gendarmes who were arresting Poles for forced labor. A few dozen of us were put in a group and taken to an unknown destination. I hinted to Felek that I couldn't let myself go on with them and had to get away. I knew that if I took off, he might be in trouble, since we had been arrested together. We agreed that, if he were asked, he would say that we had met by chance and that he didn't know me at all. I slowly began lagging behind until I was right next to the soldier at the rear. I told him I had to urinate. He allowed me. I stood still and pretended to pee. When the group and the soldier went on, I started running in the opposite direction. The German saw and shouted, "Halt!" But he didn't open fire. When I turned my head, I saw him trying to chase me, but he gave up the idea, turned around, and rejoined the group. Later I met Felek, who said the German had argued with him and threatened him, but he insisted that he didn't know me and that we had met only by chance. Because Felek was an elderly man, he was released and wasn't sent to work in Germany.

Ultimately, we didn't use the apartment because the Polish Uprising soon began.

I must also talk about the shameful and ever-present issue of informers planted among us. Such things did happen—people who worked with us became turncoats, for money or fear of the Germans. Let's go back to Krzaczek, the Pole who helped us get our people out of the Ghetto. (Krzaczek means "bush," a nickname given him, apparently, because he was short and solid.) He was a member of the AL underground whom I first met when we were preparing to get our companions out through the sewers. I learned that he had previously participated in getting our comrades out of the Többens-Schultz Area. After our trip to Lomianki Forest, I hardly ever saw him. At first there were only rumors, but soon more solid facts emerged. People said Krzaczek was a turncoat who had caused the murders of ZOB members in Warsaw and around Czestochowa. They told of a conspiracy he had made with Polish policemen. He joined to escort our arrested comrades to Czestochowa, but murdered and robbed them on the way.

Antek dealt with this issue. He informed the AL commanders, who investigated the matter and issued a death sentence against Krzaczek in absentia. We were informed of it, but the execution was left to the AL.[75]

One day, after the underground issued his death sentence, we got word that Krzaczek wanted to meet me. I hesitated and discussed my doubts with my companions, who thought I shouldn't meet him. I knew we owed him a great deal. It simply didn't make sense to me that this man, who had risked his life and helped us get our friends out of the burning Ghetto, should also have murdered our friends in cold blood for money. I decided to go see him. We met on a street in Warsaw. He had changed enormously; it was not the same Krzaczek I had known before. We walked around the streets for a long time, talking about all kinds of things. I couldn't understand what he wanted from me, despite his efforts to explain. I had the feeling the man was really starving. He begged me for cigarettes. So as not to feel blackmailed by

75. See Antek's account (Zuckerman 1993: 398–401).

him, even though I could have bought him a few packs of cigarettes, I gave him only a few, intending to find out if he would try to extort other things from me. But he didn't.

We arranged to meet again some time later, but I never saw Krzaczek again. Rumor had it that he paid with his life for an attempt to save three of our companions hiding with a concierge at Prózna Street 14. Three ZOB members there had apparently been denounced and the Gestapo went to arrest them. We don't know precisely what happened. According to one version, when the Gestapo tried to enter, our people opened fire on them and the three were killed on the spot. Another version claims that someone was taken to Gestapo headquarters. According to unsubstantiated information, it was somehow connected with Krzaczek's demise. Krzaczek, who was extraordinarily brave, apparently went to the Gestapo to learn the fate of our friends and never came out. In January 1944, all trace of him was lost.

A Warm Corner at Miodowa Street 24

In the center of the city, on bustling Miodowa Street, two young women, Inka and Marysia, lived in a one-room apartment. Inka—Dr. Inka Szwajger—worked as a pediatrician in the Jewish children's hospital in the Ghetto and moved to the Aryan side in early 1943 to live under a forged identity. Her friend Marysia—Bronka Feinmesser—had previously worked as a telephone operator in the same Jewish hospital in the Ghetto. The two of them were a few years older than me and now worked as couriers, dedicating infinite efforts and devotion to help the Jews in hiding. Their apartment also served as a meeting place for our members who were disguised as "Aryans" and lived under false names. In the thick of the various errands I performed, I would drop in on their apartment, meet with people who happened by there, hear and deliver reports.

The apartment consisted of one room on the first floor, a long corridor—the last apartment on the right. Naturally, young men came calling on two Polish girls. Staying overnight in their place presented a problem, because there was only one bed in the one room. Sometimes, when I had nowhere else to spend the night, I was forced to stay there. It was good to come there, like an oasis in the desert, where you could relax a bit. Marysia, who was optimistic and quiet by nature, created a pleasant atmosphere. Her easy-going temperament even calmed me and, I assume, the others who came there. Meeting Inka was sometimes like entering another world. It's hard to say which was nicer in that apartment—the peace and quiet, or the feeling that you could get rid of all the cares of the day. I went there a lot, but I stayed overnight only once or twice. If I didn't have to, I wouldn't bother them, since you had to be careful not to "burn" apartments. The two of them shared the only bed. When I did stay overnight, they let me sleep at their feet.

Marysia was from an assimilated family, wasn't a Zionist, and didn't know a thing about Judaism. How she came to us, I don't know. She looked like a typical Pole, spoke perfect Polish, and had big, somewhat sad blue eyes. She was always calm and didn't tend to get excited, qualities we all needed in those days. In her presence, the fear that constantly oppressed us vanished.

Marysia was the one who made contact with the group of "street children," who were later called the "Cigarette Sellers of Three Crosses Square."[76] One day we got some unsubstantiated information that a group of Jewish children was hiding in the ruins, on the Aryan side, and selling cigarettes and

76. The Cigarette Sellers were a group of Jewish children on the Aryan side of Warsaw who supported themselves by selling cigarettes. Their patron was Joseph Ziemian (Zissman). Most of them survived and immigrated to Israel. See Ziemian 1977.

newspapers. After a long investigation, we found a string that led us to Three Crosses Square, but all our attempts to make contact with the children were in vain. The group was very suspicious, and very hostile to anyone who tried to approach them. Naturally, they had good reasons. I frequently went to look at those children. My thoughts didn't tend to run in a sentimental vein; instead I considered practical means of helping them. We searched for a way to get to them and thought that, where others had failed, Marysia would succeed. Her maternal instinct did indeed help her find a way to the heart of the group, and she managed to convince them that we just wanted to help. Afterward, Marysia maintained regular contact with the children, meeting them and giving them advice and money. She also provided them with forged papers. This went on until the Polish Uprising began.

6 Underground Operations

Where Are the Jews from Pawiak?

Luba, known as "Green Marysia," longed to get involved in underground work. We had grave reservations about using people who served as a cover for other comrades. If Luba were to be caught, the apartment registered in her name would be "burned" and those hiding in it would become prey for the Gestapo. However, Luba and Irka wanted to take part in ZOB activities. There were only a few of us, it was too hard for us to perform all the missions, and here were two pretty girls who looked "good" and wanted to act. So from time to time I threw caution to the winds and assigned them various errands.

In 1944, near the start of the Polish Uprising, we got word that a group of Jews had escaped from Pawiak, the prison next to the former Ghetto, and I was assigned to check it out. I was given an address on Zlota Street, where I was supposed to get more detailed information and meet people who would take me to the escapees. The whole thing looked suspicious to me: I was worried that it might be a Gestapo trap. I asked Luba to accompany me. Her job was to follow me and watch so that she could return quickly and report to Antek if anything happened to me. Luba walked a few dozen meters behind me. As agreed, she stayed in the street while I went up to the apartment. A blond woman and two men were there. A discussion—or rather, an argument—started, which smelled like blackmail. They began telling me about the Jews who had escaped from Pawiak. They said they knew where the escapees were and were willing to take me to them, but in exchange, various intermediaries had to be paid. On the spot I decided to go for broke: I pulled out my pistol with a dramatic gesture, put it on the table in front of me, and said,

"As a member of the AK, I must tell you that it is our human obligation to help those who escaped from prison. Poles should be expected to cooperate fully in this case, but you are trying to set conditions. I am not willing to do that. I demand your immediate cooperation, or else—we will give you a short trial!" The threat worked: they changed their tune in a twinkling. One of the men immediately promised to take me to where the escapees were hiding. I said, "I should inform you that the house is surrounded by my comrades, so I suggest you don't try any tricks, because you are liable to pay a high price for it."

We went down to the street. Although we had a long way to go, I refused to ride, as he suggested, and insisted that we go on foot so Luba could follow me. From time to time I would turn my head to see if she was there. The man led me to Wola, a neighborhood notorious for its underworld denizens, where most of the houses were small and rickety. Meanwhile, I turned my head around, looked here and there, and didn't see Luba. I imagined it was because we were walking too fast. I was aware that I was in great danger. We were walking on a crowded street, but every stranger—like me—was conspicuous. Nevertheless, I was sure I had to play out the game. Finally, my escort stopped and pointed to a nearby house, "They should be here." Finding no one in the house, I asked for an explanation. "Looks like they had to be transferred somewhere else," the man replied. I decided it was time to retreat with honor. "You go back to the city with me," I told him. "On the way we'll decide how we're going to take care of it." At that moment my entire being was focused on one thought: how to get out of that neighborhood to the center of the city, where I would feel safer and know my way around better.

When we got to the center of the city, I suggested another meeting the next day, so he could find out where the escapees from Pawiak were. He solemnly promised to do so, and we parted with a handshake, like old friends. His story may have been a complete fabrication, or he may not have been in on the secret of the affair and just wanted money. In any case, he obviously didn't suspect I was a Jew, or else the neighborhood thugs would have killed me at a hint from him. When I met Luba, I teased her, jokingly: "Look, I gave you a simple job and you didn't do it. How can I give you serious missions?" To this very day that memory bothers her, for no reason.

The name Pawiak didn't drop off the agenda. Rumors persisted that Jews were still in the prison—Jews from Greece brought to deal with the corpses scattered around the Ghetto and to collect whatever property had wound up there. I was told that two Jews, escaped prisoners from Pawiak, were hiding in the town of Grodzisk. While in prison, they had worked in maintenance and so knew the place and how to get in and out of it. Luba had "protectees" in Grodzisk whom she visited, and I thought the simplest thing would be to send her to bring the two Jews, Krupnik and Domb, to Warsaw. She brought Krupnik with her on the train. As soon as she got to the apartment at Panska 5, she said another hasty goodbye to her boyfriend, Jurek Grossberg. She explained that she had promised Domb and his wife to find the Polish family in Praga who were keeping their daughter and to bring the little girl to them in Grodzisk. While she was in Praga, the Polish Uprising began, and Luba got stuck there; all her attempts to cross the river with the child were foiled by heavy battles. When the Uprising began, our companions moved to Leszno 18 and left Jurek alone at Panska 5. Fighting raged all around. After it died down, our friends hurried to the apartment and found the building destroyed. We learned that Jurek had apparently left the apartment and been killed in the street by members of the right wing of the AK, who were dreadful anti-Semites; Jurek looked very Jewish and had been caught as soon as he came out. If Luba had known her boyfriend was in danger, she would certainly have refused to go on the errand I had assigned to her.

Here I may say that every single operation was weighed individually. Once I was convinced it was vital, I would assign it to others or take it on myself. One operation I wanted to assign to myself was, however, of dubious importance. I recall the argument between me and my companions on May Day 1944, exactly one year from the night I came out of the Ghetto to scout a path of evacuation. I was always armed with at least one pistol, and usually I carried two. Why? "Because two are better than one." Let's not examine the logic too carefully. I told my friends at Panska 5 that I was going out, that I felt like shooting a German so he'd feel May Day and the Germans wouldn't stroll around the streets like lords. My friends attacked and scolded me, demanding that I behave rationally and show more consideration for others.

Attempt to Establish a New Fighting Group

In the spring and summer of 1944 we were busy, among other things, with an attempt to establish a fighting group among the Jews hiding in and around Warsaw. The ZOB assigned me to get in touch with the AK instructor who would train the group. So I had to go through the hiding places to "pull out" candidates for the battle group. Some of those hiding weren't organized by the ZOB; they were "ordinary Jews" who had managed to get out of the Ghetto and find a place on the Aryan side. Business as usual went on in Warsaw. The Germans had long ago pronounced the city *Judenrein,* and they believed their own declarations. The Poles enjoyed relative freedom and led more or less normal lives. Only for the thousands of Jews who lived in hiding or with false identities was danger constantly lurking. I went from one hideout to another looking for candidates for the new battle group. I ignored the rules of caution, seeking people who were not my "protectees" but who were just as brave and steadfast as members of the organization. Cooped up for months in their niches, closets, and attics, these people had succeeded in preserving the human values they believed in. Some of them couldn't even come out at night to breathe fresh air on the roof or balcony. You had to be doubly careful in contacting them, and I was very anxious when I dared talk with such a "strange" Jew about organization and fighting.

The AK gave us an instructor who had formerly served in the Polish army. He had professional knowledge and a talent for communicating it briefly. He was one of my sources of information about what was going on in the Polish underground. From my contact with him, I began to understand that the Poles were thinking seriously about an uprising, preparing to expel the German occupiers from their capital—and perhaps from all of Poland. We sensed the uprising approaching, but we didn't know an exact date. The atmosphere in the Warsaw streets changed completely in those weeks. You no longer saw German soldiers patrolling alone; they walked only in groups. More and more German soldiers were attacked and stripped of their weapons in the city streets. In the past the Germans would have caught a few dozen people at random and executed them at the scene of the incident. But at that time, for some reason, they overlooked such events. The mood in the street improved, and of course we felt better too. We thought our troubles would soon be over. Underground information said that the Russians were approaching and that the vanguard of the Red Army was already forty or fifty kilometers from Warsaw, not far from the suburb of Praga.

In July 1944 I was living with Irka in a summer resort on the Otwock train line south of Warsaw. When we learned that the uprising was about to begin, we caught the last train from Otwock to be with our companions in Warsaw. In the circumstances, I didn't have time to activate the fighting group.

7 The Polish Uprising

The Uprising Comes Suddenly

On my return to Warsaw, I found myself near the impressive courthouse between Ogrodowa and Leszno streets, where all the courts of the capital had been concentrated in 1939. The street looked different: you didn't see housewives carrying shopping bags or officials rushing to work; and you could feel something in the air, a tension steeped in exaltation. I saw a group of real fighters holding weapons—not in uniform but wearing armbands—approach in what looked like battle formation. After so many years, to see Poles holding weapons in broad daylight! At that moment, I blurted out a juicy Polish curse. Without thinking very much, I made a decision on the spot to join the AK fighting group that was attacking the big office building where the Germans were well fortified. There weren't many men in the attack group. In just a few minutes, the first casualty occurred: a young man I didn't know was shot in the head and collapsed. We tried unsuccessfully to penetrate the building a few times, and an hour or so later the iron gate suddenly opened and the Germans dashed off in an armored car. We entered, waving the Polish flag, and turned the place into district headquarters of the Armia Krajowa. I joined an elite unit consisting mainly of former army men, most of them officers. They gave me the uniform of a Polish policeman, a hat, and a red-and-white armband with the letters AK—the only identification of the rebels.

Life at the base began to be organized: the fighters were divided into units and every unit took responsibility for a sector of the city. There were also special units whose major function was to provide first aid and supplies. The building was quite new and well built—a fortress. I recall that one of the groups was sent into action; they said they were going to liberate prisoners. The first hours of the uprising were a time of elation. Shots were heard all around, everything breathed an atmosphere of popular rebellion. Solemn proclamations were issued, like "Everyone to arms!" and "Expel the enemy!" In my innocence, I thought we were close to release from the German yoke. Nevertheless, I kept quiet about who I really was and retained my false identity.

Irena Gelblum (Irka) was with me. I sat in the courthouse and my soul went out to my companions. As long as operations were going on, things were pushed out of my consciousness and I forgot; but when we sat idle, I felt a desire to go to my friends. I knew that most of them were at Leszno Street 18, where there was a well-built hideout behind a brick wall that you entered through a coal stove. The innovation was that the entire fire chamber could be removed, so you could crawl in through the opening. Bolek (Haim Ellenbogen), a Polish professional named Woyciechowski, and I had prepared the apartment for this purpose. After we left Panska 5, Zivia, Tuvia, Sak, Stefan, and a few other friends moved here, where the archives of the Dror movement and the ZOB were concentrated. Of all the apartment hiding places, I thought this one was the best; it served both as a hideout and as a base of operations. I decided to see what was happening with our friends at Leszno 18. I did indeed find them—all of them. The apartment was crowded and their weapons were no longer hidden.

Under such circumstances arguments often erupted, especially since the group included public figures and leaders of different movements who had been thrown together by chance in those tense and stormy days. One argument had to do with which of the two undergrounds we should join, the Armia Krajowa or the Armia Ludowa (AL). There was no question of whether we should join the uprising, since we were a fighting group and had a commander, Antek. He was our liaison with the command staffs of both organizations. Aside from the ZOB, the Jewish National Committee also maintained direct contact with the two undergrounds. At the top level contact among the organizations was regular, but it became more sporadic at the lower levels.

"For Your Freedom and Ours"

We argued about joining in light of the fact that the AK had told us nothing about their plans for an uprising, but we had picked things up in the street. As I said, in early 1944 the AK appealed to us to form a Jewish unit, which they would train, to take part in operations when the time came. Then the AK disappeared, leaving us in doubt about whether to join them. Some of our members argued against cooperating with the AK because it was an extremely right-wing organization controlled by General Rydz-Smigly's people.[77] Nor did we get reliable information about the participation of the AL underground in the uprising. Later it turned out that the AL didn't participate at all in the planning and consequently was cut off from the weapons depots as soon as the fighting erupted.

In the end Antek and I were assigned to negotiate with the command staff of the AL in Starówka (the Old City). I went to check out the route to the meeting place. The rebels had captured groups of buildings in the city and held "islands of resistance." The Germans were supposed to be everywhere else, but there were a lot of no-man's-lands. Sometimes, on the same street, Germans and rebels alternated, with no-man's-lands scattered here and there. On our way to Starówka we passed through streets where life seemed to be going on as usual. Pedestrians, surprised at seeing anyone, hurried off.

77. Marshal Edward Rydz-Smigly, chief of the Polish armed forces just before they were defeated in World War II.

It was easy to find the AL headquarters because of the flag waving over it and the dozens of fighters milling around outside. It was a heartening sight: fear of the Germans had obviously disappeared. We were taken to a room on the ground floor, where people in civilian clothes were sitting at tables. Our discussion with the members of the Armia Ludowa was brief and to the point; there was no need for introductions on either side. They accepted the fighting group of the ZOB into their service on the spot. Antek was appointed commander not only of our group but of all Jews who might join the uprising. Moreover, a Major Nestek was appointed to serve as liaison with us. (Only after the war did I learn his real name, Menashe Matiewicki, and discover his Jewish origin.)[78]

In coordination with the AL command staff, we issued an appeal to all Jews hiding in and around Warsaw to join the general uprising. When the discussion ended, Antek and I returned to Leszno 18, reported to our companions, and organized for the departure to Starówka. The apartment at Leszno 18 was closed and abandoned. At the start of the uprising the AL didn't want to assign us to purely operational functions. Since there were only a handful of us left, and since we were the last of the ZOB, they explained that they felt obligated to protect us.[79] However, we insisted on performing the same functions as all the other fighters, and they granted our request. Our group was posted in the sector whose central axis crossed Freta Street and almost bordered the Wisla River. We had to locate our own positions, but they weren't hard to find, since most of the buildings were empty. Once again the fighters were resisting the Germans, who were a few hundred meters away from our positions. They didn't try to break through, but merely fired cannon shells or light ammunition at us now and then.

78. See Zuckerman 1993: 540.
79. See Zuckerman 1993: 534.

I continued as a member of the fighting unit of the AK based in the courthouse building and maintained daily contact with the ZOB members in Starówka.

The rebels carried the first three days of the uprising, and morale was very high. Food supplies were regular and even the weather was good. Our victory seemed assured, and the war appeared about to end for us. The change in mood began on the afternoon of the third day, when the Germans began aerial bombing of the areas captured by the rebels. They split the areas in two and surrounded some of the rebel units. In other places, German areas were surrounded by the rebels. In any event, communication between rebel centers was disrupted and the morale of the fighters declined. The AL followed accepted practice in the Polish army: its main operations involved protecting defensive positions to prevent the Germans from occupying the territories that had fallen into rebel hands. The rebels didn't initiate offensive operations.

One day as I was lying down in the AK base in the courthouse, I picked up snatches of a conversation among my fellow fighters. They said that the situation was grave and that we had to think about escaping to the forests in eastern Poland. As a first stop they mentioned Lomianki Forest, not far from Warsaw. My ears pricked up. I don't think they meant to hide anything from me, but they were friends, whereas I was new and foreign to them. They also may have thought I was sleeping and didn't think it necessary to wake me. Naturally, it didn't occur to them that I was a Jew. As the conversation progressed, I realized they had concluded that the uprising was doomed to failure and that it would be stupid to go on; it was better to escape while there was still time. I didn't believe my ears, and when I felt the conversation was coming to an end, I got up and sat with them. In the unit I was called Glina (that is, Mud), a nickname that stuck to me because of the color of the uniform I wound up with. "Glina's up," they said, and suggested I join the escape. I took the floor and said, "Gentlemen, how could you think of running away from the battle, after only a few hours of fighting? Are you willing to admit to failure, to retreat and abandon your companions in this building and, as a result, the whole quarter? Why, the Jews in the Ghetto, who fought with fewer and worse weapons than ours for weeks, are better than us." My speech had an influence: the plans for escape were abandoned and they agreed to continue.

The next morning I stood guard in the street outside the courtyard of the building. Each watch normally lasted six hours, but I stood for more than fifteen hours and no one came to replace me. I was on the verge of collapse, battling fatigue, and from time to time I dozed off. At last my patience ran out and I shouted for a replacement. It turned out that while I was standing guard an order had come to leave the building. Irena and I went to our comrades at AL headquarters to report on the situation; then we returned to the courthouse to find out what was going on. We were told that an immediate withdrawal had been ordered and that, lacking vehicles to evacuate the wounded, they had decided to leave them in the cellar to the mercy of the Germans. Only a few nurses had volunteered to stay with them.

During my time in the AK fighting unit, I encountered shocking phenomena. One day Irena and I were scouting near Iron Gate Square, where German shelling had burned down the market. As we approached, we saw a large group of people in prisoners' uniforms being pushed into the burning buildings by armed members of the AK, who ordered them to pull the food stored there out of the fire. I had a camera and took several pictures of that vicious act, but unfortunately I later lost them. As I came closer, I learned that the prisoners were Hungarian Jews who had been brought to Warsaw as laborers by the Germans. During the uprising they were "freed" by AK fighters, only to be forced to perform dangerous and humiliating functions. I went to the commander of the AK unit and told him I saw no point to his behavior and asked why he thought the wretched prisoners had to risk their lives for us. I took advantage of the fact that we rebels had no insignia of rank. In the great confusion you couldn't know if you were talking to someone whose rank was higher or lower than yours. When I raised my voice aggressively, the commander started worrying about his hide and left the prisoners alone.

Later Irena and I left the AK altogether, went over to the AL, and joined my ZOB companions in Starówka. I told them about the incident I had witnessed and we decided to try to get the Jews away from the AK, which would surely make things easier for them because of our contacts. I estimated that there were fifty people in the group. We negotiated with the key people in the AK and learned about other groups of Jewish prisoners in their hands. Our objective was both to save the prisoners from the AK and to gain reinforcements for our own fighters. The Poles agreed in principle to transfer the Jewish prisoners to us, but our attempt to rescue them failed because of a break in contact, the difficulties of transfer, and the prevailing chaos.

Before I joined the AL, Irena and I returned to the courthouse area to make a few arrangements and to say good-bye to my companions there. A tremendous stream of people was moving in the opposite direction. We were told that the Germans were attacking the area and that everyone was leaving. We had great difficulty clearing a path to the courthouse, and I found it in the final stages of abandonment. Disorder prevailed; people were running back and forth, and no one really knew what was going on. I didn't find my AK companions, but I did meet a woman I had known who, with much feeling, took a medallion of the Holy Mother of Czestochowa from around her neck and gave it to me to protect me from harm. I tried to get away, but the woman pleaded with me to take it. Finally we made our way back to Starówka, to join our comrades who were already in the ranks of the AL.

From Starówka to Leszno 18

The situation rapidly deteriorated. The Germans closed in on us from all sides. Clearly, the hope that the Russians would cross the Wisla and rush to the aid of the rebels had no basis in reality. Sense and sensibility said that the uprising was doomed to failure. Antek and I were summoned to the headquarters of the sector, where I was requested, as an experienced person, to mark a retreat route through the sewers. My instructions were to scout out a passageway to the Warsaw suburb of Zolibórz.

I was placed in charge of a unit of mainly sergeants and officers who had served in the Polish army, all of them much older than me. After a briefing, we set the date of the reconnaissance mission. I felt uncomfortable commanding older men, especially since I had never served in a regular army. Therefore, I talked to one of the fighters of the unit, and we agreed that he would be the ostensible commander as far as the men were concerned; I would lead them through him. At the set time we descended into the sewers. After reconnoitering for a few hours, I fixed the route and gave the men a precise explanation of where we would emerge in Zolibórz. I had made prolonged observations through the manhole cover, which was partly covered with a grating, and had noted its exact location. On our way back we marked the path with chalk. The experience I had acquired when we brought our companions out of the destroyed Ghetto helped me find my way.

I returned to headquarters and reported on the completion of the mission. Later, after leaving Starówka, I learned that the rebels had indeed used the escape route I had marked, since they could no longer hold out in the Old City. Those who escaped to Zolibórz with the AL fighters included a ZOB group left in Starówka.

One day Antek and Zivia called me to one of the posts, and Antek ordered me to lead a group of comrades out of the sector to our previous base at Leszno 18. Seeing amazement on my face, he explained that it was because of his faith in me. "Look around," he said, "who can I depend on?" He added that the movement archive was on Leszno Street and that there were important documents and publications that had to be protected by any means. Finally, he read me the names of those who were going with me. I was furious, since the list included all those who were "unfit" to fight. Moreover, I thought the operation was crazy, since, according to our information, the house on Leszno Street was either already occupied by the Germans or, at best, was in no-man's-land. Either way, to get there we had to cross the front lines. There was very little chance we'd make it. And why endanger ourselves? For papers? For "history"? I objected and argued bitterly. To this day I argue with myself over this issue. But it never occurred to me not to obey Antek's order. I organized the people. Major Natek, of the AL command staff, joined us to take us through the front lines. I held onto my revolver. My heart was filled with rage.[80]

80. Author's note: Since this issue still bothers me, I asked friends who control Antek's estate to release part of his testimony that deals with this matter: "At the meeting of the AL staff, I suggested we try to set up basic links in the rear—Leszno wasn't yet captured by the Germans—where we could take all those who weren't needed. I told them there was an extraordinary bunker at Leszno 18, and I suggested we send mostly girls there, Polish and Jewish girls. It was important to set up a base in that building, in my bunker, if need be. If we had to withdraw—there would be a place to withdraw to. And then, from that house, we would go forward until we got out of Warsaw. . . . The staff understood . . . this conception. For that rea-

We left at sundown, and it was dark when we got to the rebel front lines. Major Natek identified himself and we were given permission to proceed to the German lines. It turned out that Leszno 18 was in no-man's-land. The area was shrouded in flames and, except for us, not a soul was moving toward the Germans. While walking, Major Natek tried to persuade us to turn around. He repeated his plea several times as we went forward and the situation in the area grew worse. I had initially refused to go to Leszno Street, but having gotten this far, I didn't intend to go back. In my argument with the major, I used the Polish saying: Only a goat goes backward.

Walking in the streets, past the burning ruins, was a dreadful experience. We crossed passageways, cleared a path into blazing houses. Except for the light from the fires, it was pitch-dark, and at any minute we were liable to fall into a German ambush or hit on a German position. We reached Leszno 18 after midnight; the Germans entered the courtyard of the house shortly after.

In Flames and Cellars

German shouts rang out, ordering the inhabitants to leave their apartments and report to the courtyard. We consulted on the spot and decided to stay inside. The Germans repeated the announcement twice more, warning that the house would be destroyed along with all the occupants. Nevertheless, we didn't move. We heard band music played by German soldiers in the yard: was that the signal to start the operation? This is one of my strangest memories: everything around going up in flames, walls caving in—and that music.

---

son, we sent a group to Leszno. . . . Kazik was very vital to us—a fighter, but he knew the bunker and we counted on his being able to organize things." (See Zuckerman 1993: 469 [ed.].)

Through the window I saw the players blowing into their instruments, and I stood still, hypnotized. Walls were collapsing, people were being killed, and there they stood and played. . . . A few seconds later, the building was set on fire by flamethrowers and went up in a blaze. Smoke penetrated the apartment and it was hard to breathe.

We ran to a lower floor and entered an apartment that had been broken open. What with the rising smoke and the commotion, I lost part of the group. Irena, Marysia, and perhaps Stefan stayed with me. The others—Yosef Sak, Stasia, and Krysia—disappeared. We found rags and water in the apartment. We soaked the rags and put them over our faces to make it easier to breathe. We took off our clothes so they wouldn't catch fire. The whole time the Germans stood in the courtyard and continued to play.

Could we hold out until they left? As soon as they did, we would try to break out of the burning house. A few minutes later the Germans could no longer stand the heat in the U-shaped courtyard and went out into the street. At the very last minute, when it was impossible to bear the heat anymore, we tried to burst out through the wooden staircase. But the staircase was burning and there was no way to get through. The only thing left to do was to jump out of a second-story window into the courtyard. The first to jump was Marysia, who had been a famous athlete in Warsaw before the war. She landed safely and the rest of us followed. The courtyard was all ablaze; we didn't know where to turn. If we went out into the street, it would clearly be the end of us.

Instead, we looked for a hiding place in the burning building. In one corner we saw a brick structure that served as a public lavatory. Amazingly, it was still standing and we went inside for protection. There we found a cover over the opening of the cistern, which was big enough for us to enter and huddle against one another. Once we were inside, we put the cover back in its place. Irka, Marysia, and I sat like that for a few hours—it was hard to estimate how long. All of a sudden I felt a terrible pain in my eyes, which kept getting worse. I felt as if I were going blind. (Blindness can be caused by the accumulation of gasses in a cistern.) We didn't have any water to wash our eyes, but the girls were clever: they stroked my head, leaned over me one after the other, and licked my eyes. That gave me a little relief, perhaps only because I sensed they were taking care of me.

Some time later we heard noises. First we thought they were human footsteps right on top of us, and we kept silent. But when the noises came back, we concluded that they weren't human footsteps but objects occasionally falling down with a dull thud. We were afraid the house would collapse on top of us. We moved the cover to check on the situation and to clear a path so as not to be buried under the rubble. It was afternoon. It turned out that we had been in the cistern for more than twenty-four hours. I looked around outside and we went out into the courtyard. Smoke was still rising from the house. We searched for any hiding place at all. Suddenly someone called us—Yosef Sak and Stasia, who were hiding in one of the cellars of the building. We entered the cellar through the window. They were lying exhausted, their faces on the floor, trying to breathe air that was a bit cooler. The other members of our group, who had been separated from us during the panic of the fire, were also hiding in the cellar. We gathered together to decide what to do. A glance outside made it clear that the area was swarming with Germans. All we could do was to prepare for a long stay in the cellar.

Our first major problem was a lack of water, and then we found a barrel of water in the courtyard—maybe it was rainwater—which kept us alive for at least two weeks, because we rationed ourselves to a quarter-cup a day. Then we began exploring the cellar, and fortunately we found food and even cigarettes. The inhabitants of the building had hoarded delicacies like sausage, oil, flour, rice, and even clothes. How-

ever, our basic problem was the lack of water, so we decided
to dig a well in the cellar.

The Germans had camped in the church next door, using
it as headquarters for that section of the front. We heard the
conversations that went on there and the orders that were
issued. As time went on, the Germans heard strange sounds
coming from the rubble and began to suspect that somebody
was hiding there. Or perhaps it was simply the curiosity of
soldiers, eager to search for things in abandoned buildings.
Now and then German units burst in and searched the courtyard and the building. Luckily, they didn't come down to us.

While we were in the cellar, on one of my reconnaissance
expeditions I found a German announcement addressed to
any Poles in hiding, calling on them to surrender and leave
the area. I thought about it and decided that we would do
well to obey. I knew very well that the Germans treated Poles
differently from Jews; and I knew that, if we turned ourselves
in, we could expect to be sent to a labor camp near Warsaw
and not to a death camp. I suggested to my companions that
we leave the cellar, report to the soldiers, and present the
announcement—in short, turn ourselves in. They refused to
take such a step, seeing it as anathema to their beliefs,
whereas I knew that death was lurking for us here at every
moment. We had a lively argument, and they even accused
me of being defeatist. Some were silent and didn't express
any opinion. My major opponent was my friend Yosef Sak,
who was much older than me. The argument lasted several
days. Ultimately, I said I was willing to leave the cellar by
myself, but on second thought I decided not to abandon my
friends.

Weeks passed. All that time we kept digging a well in the
cellar. One day, as I was digging in the pit, which was more
than two meters deep—the first drops were already visible in
the ground—Krysia, who was our lookout, suddenly called

an alarm: "The Germans are coming into the cellar!" In a wink I was out of the pit, but my companions had put out the lights, forgotten me, and taken off. I didn't know where to turn. How had they run off in the darkness? Suddenly, someone grabbed my hand and pulled me along. It was Irena, who had kept her head and come to my aid. We got out to another cellar on the other side of the building and rejoined our friends. We decided to continue hiding as long as we could.

The Allies were now bombing the area at night. Despite the danger, we came out of the cellar to watch the shelling of the German positions. We were overjoyed, but also increasingly sure that we couldn't hide for long, that the Germans would ultimately discover us. We agreed that, when the time came, we would declare that there were women in our group, and that Marysia and Irka would go out first to calm the Germans and keep them from shooting. Meanwhile, Yosef Sak told us that he intended to commit suicide with some potassium cyanide he had, but I didn't let him carry out his plan. I told him, "None of us has potassium cyanide, and you will share our fate. You're no better than we are." I was the only one with a pistol. I decided I would go out last. If the Germans didn't open fire, I would hide the pistol in the cellar.

Things did indeed go according to that scenario, more or less. When the Germans came within a few meters and there was no more hope that they wouldn't find us, I signaled to the girls, who shouted, "There are women here. Don't shoot!" We formed a line and the surprised soldiers shouted, "Come out!" The rest of us followed the girls out; I was the last. The soldiers were stunned to see a group of live people, but it didn't occur to them that we were Jews. Our assumption that they wouldn't doubt they were dealing with Polish Christians was borne out. The soldiers, who weren't German but Ukrainian, were interested in the jewels the women were wearing. Irka took off a bracelet in the form of a serpent, which I had found in one of the cellars and given her. Marysia and Stasia gave them other jewelry. I told them there was a mandolin in one of the cellars, and I even offered to go down with them. After they had gathered up various things in the cellar, they said they would take us to an assembly station where Poles were being sent out of Warsaw. They ordered us to follow them.

We went out to the street. Soldiers were posted at every other house, and as we walked behind the Ukrainian soldiers, an SS man stopped us and asked them who we were. They tried to tell him the circumstances of our arrest, but they stammered, and Yosef Sak translated their words into German. Suddenly, the SS man pointed to Sak and Stasia and shouted, "*Jude! Jude!*" and ordered the escort to take us to Ukrainian headquarters. When we realized they were taking us to the headquarters of the Ukrainian unit and not to the civilian assembly station, some of us decided not to go. The cruelty and sadism of the Ukrainians were well known, and we were afraid of rape and harsh tortures. Some appealed to the SS man to kill them on the spot. I managed to keep my aplomb. My guiding thought was that there was no need to rush to die, and I succeeded in convincing my companions not to hurry into it. I dragged Irena and Marysia by force. The SS man left us. An artillery battle was going on between the Russians and the Germans. Soldiers were everywhere. I saw there was no chance of running away or finding a hiding place.

When we got to the street corner and had to go toward Ukrainian headquarters, as the SS man had ordered, the soldiers refused to let us cross, arguing that a battle was taking place. According to them, the area was completely surrounded, a *kessel* (cauldron) in their language, something like a closed barrel—meaning that nothing goes in and nothing comes out. An argument ensued between the escort and the soldiers, with Sak translating. Sak, who also maintained his aplomb all the way, displayed initiative and quick-mindedness: he "arranged" his translations to tip the balance in our favor. Finally, an order came to take us to the assembly station, and thus we returned to our original plan.

The station was a church on Wolska Street. Warsaw had been destroyed, and what remained were primarily the churches. As we walked, we discussed the situation and decided that as soon as we got to the church, we would scatter through the crowd so as not to be an easily identifiable group. A few minutes later we reached the assembly station. The Ukrainians turned us over to a German patrol, who took us inside. There, as agreed, we separated from one another. A large crowd was gathered in the church—children, women, and even men. They were sitting, talking, and waiting for orders from the Germans. Soon after we came, a German officer entered and asked about the "group brought from Leszno Street." None of us responded. The German officer began searching in the crowd. When he got to Sak, he asked him his name; Sak gave a very Polish name, of course. The officer asked, "How long have you had that name?" The same thing happened when he came to Stasia—obviously, he suspected the two of them. Finally, he left them and went on his way. An order was quickly given for us to line up. Those gathered in the church had to go outside, line up, and march to the railroad station! We had expected that order. We mingled with the crowd and marched to the station, where we were ordered to get into the passenger cars.

When the train began to move, we felt great relief, a sense of having been saved—this time. To this day it's hard for me to understand why Sak and Stasia weren't arrested, even though the officer suspected they were Jews. Perhaps the Germans didn't have time for that, since their army was already in a general rout. The whole incident didn't last long. We were captured close to noon, and by one o'clock we were on the train. That same afternoon we got to the transit camp in Pruszków.

8 The ZOB Back in Action

Pruszków and Suchedniów

We were taken to a camp populated by several thousand Warsaw residents, who had been taken out of their homes and sent there at the height of the uprising. Acquaintances we encountered in the camp gave us a picture of the German procedure: young people were sent to forced labor in Germany; old people, women, and children were released.

I don't remember how long I was in Pruszków. One morning we were ordered to line up for classification. Hundreds of human beings had to parade in front of German officers, who decided whom to release and whom to send to labor camp. As we stood in line, our whole group assembled. We hadn't agreed whether to try to escape or to join the group sent to Germany for labor, thus putting an end to our constant danger. Stasia and Krysia decided they didn't have the strength to go on living under such awful tension and preferred to go work in Germany. As for Stefan and Sak, their chances of staying in Poland were good because of their age. My own memory is a blur. As I recall, a mood of apathy descended on me. I was fed up with the whole thing. I imagined that it would be better for me to go to Germany, but Stefan, Irka, and Marysia coaxed me into changing my mind.

Irka and I were classified among those going to Germany. But a moment later the two of us managed to slip out and join a group of women and children waiting to be released. We weren't suspected of being Jews. The women helped us and hid us in their midst; apparently they took us for members of the Polish underground.

When we got onto the train, we "kept a low profile" with the help of the other passengers. The Germans passed through the cars, looking for people who should have been sent for forced labor. The train moved. At dusk we got to Suchedniów, where we were released.

I had known the city previously. Before the Polish Uprising, I had been in touch with a Polish laborer who worked nearby, in a German ammunition plant in Skarzysko-Kamienna, where Jewish forced laborers were also working. The Pole had once helped the ZOB make contact with the Jews; he had come to us in Warsaw a few times, where we would meet and arrange things as we walked the streets. I had also visited his home on several occasions.

We arrived in Suchedniów with nothing—no means of livelihood, no documents (we had lost them in the uprising). We needed immediate help. The Pole recognized us and did not hesitate to assist us. First of all, he found Sak a place to live and we invented a "cover" for him: we spread a story in town that Sak was a high-ranking Polish officer. Sak was an imposing figure, a professor of Polish literature who knew whole books by heart, but his facial features were liable to get him turned in. We didn't want any danger and the story we planted among the inhabitants took root. Everyone kept the secret.

I suggested we try to make contact with the members of the underground in Krakow. In the past I had visited the city to create contact with our people in Plaszow Camp. I knew people there who were active in the organization to help the Jews. One of them was a Polish Christian named Zegota; another was a woman called Marysia Marianska (a Jew, now Miriam Peleg). The writer Bartoszewski also worked in that organization in Krakow and Warsaw.

A few days after we arrived in Suchedniów, Marysia and Irka were sent to Krakow to ask for help in arranging for documents and money. I thought it wouldn't take more than a few days, but it didn't work out according to my schedule. Three days went by, another day, then one more, and still the women hadn't returned. I decided to send a messenger after them to find out what had happened. I recruited the thirteen-year-old son of the Polish worker who was our host. He was a smart boy. I gave him the necessary instructions and asked him, if need be, to perform the errand that had been assigned to Marysia and Irka.

As I accompanied the boy, I saw a group of about a hundred prisoners near the train—Red Army soldiers, led by a few SS men. The prisoners looked hungry and desperate; their clothing was in tatters. Peasants who gathered to gaze took pity on them and tossed them some raw potatoes. The prisoners fell on the potatoes like animals battling for crumbs of food. The Germans imposed order with their rifle butts. At that moment I thought how low a human being can be brought by hunger.

The boy managed to get in touch with the people in Krakow. Obviously, getting hold of the supplies and organizing had taken more time than I had figured, since all the official forms had required forged documents. Finally, the girls also returned, bringing everything necessary to prepare documents as well as money. It was impossible to make proper documents in Krakow because there weren't any photos, so they brought the whole "workshop" to us, along with Marysia Marianska.

In Suchedniów, Marysia Marianska forged not only *Kennkarte* but also *Arbeitskarte*, documents testifying to registration in the industrial service, which also served as confirmation that the bearer was employed as a laborer. She got to work at once and made documents for all of us. After she finished, I decided to go to Krakow with her to try to renew ZOB operations. Contact with other members of the ZOB had been disrupted when we separated in the Old City of Warsaw and I was sent to Leszno 18. As I was about to leave for Krakow, Irena and Marysia Marianska joined me. On the way to the railroad station I saw a woman telling fortunes with cards. I approached her and asked what fate she saw for me. Among other things, she said, "I advise you not to travel on the next train to Krakow." Nevertheless, I and the two women boarded the train, and at one of the stations German gendarmes took me off along with all the other young men.

We were taken to a jail that served as a transit camp for shipment to Germany. I was in a group of Poles. I escaped only thanks to the courage of the two beautiful girls. Claiming that I was their relative and that they were willing to give "a lot" for my release, they promised to meet the Germans that night. I saw them standing there, coaxing and weeping. This went on for a while, and from time to time more groups of men were brought to the courtyard. Finally, the Germans gave in and released me. We managed to get away and, as the Germans waited for their dates, got on the train that brought us to Krakow without further incident.

In Krakow—and a Sortie to the Partisans

Marysia found us a place to live with the wife of a Polish officer who was a prisoner of war. We stayed there a few weeks. One day I went to meet Michal Borwicz, who was hiding under an assumed name and serving as district commander in the Polish underground.[81] I knew about him from my previous visit, before the Polish Uprising.

I was given careful instructions for contacting Borwicz. In such a case, you must find the meeting place solely according to your directions, so as not to arouse suspicion by asking questions. I took the train to a certain station and continued on foot. It was afternoon and I was alone in the area. I entered

81. Michal Borwicz, a Polish Jewish writer, was one of the organizers of the underground in Yanov Camp in Lvov. He escaped to Krakow with the help of Polish contacts and commanded a partisan unit of the Polish Socialist party in the Miechów area. He survived the war and later died in Paris.

a house I identified from the directions I had been given. Inside I met a woman and gave her the password. (It was usually a sentence that wouldn't make listeners suspicious, something like, "When does the next train leave?" or, "How do you get to such-and-such a place?") I saw hesitation in her eyes. She avoided a clear answer. "My husband will be back in a little while, and then we'll talk," she said. I must admit that I doubted I had come to the right place, but various signs indicated that it was. I decided to wait until the man of the house returned. A few minutes later he came in from the field. We shook hands. I gave him the password; he didn't answer, but just left the room. I didn't understand what it meant. Nevertheless, I waited. The man quickly came back and beckoned me into another room, where I found the man I wanted to see. Borwicz told me that when a strange person was seen approaching the house, he would get up, climb out the window, and hide under a heap of straw next to the house. Not until the man of the house signaled that everything was all right did he return to the room—back through the window.

Borwicz invited me to go out to the field with him. The weather was nice and we stayed in the barn for several hours. We told each other what had happened since our last meeting. He invited me to attend a meeting of his fighting unit that evening, and I was delighted to accept. In the evening a few dozen men assembled for a preparatory meeting with the commander. A discussion began and my neighbors to the right and left wanted to bring me in. Among other things, fictional tales were told about the magnitude of the battles in the Warsaw Ghetto and other absurdities. I avoided expressing my opinion so as not to arouse suspicion, since no one knew I was a Jew. The next day I returned to Krakow.

One day they took me off the train along with other Poles and led us to a Gestapo station. Our papers were examined thoroughly. The Germans wanted to see our Kennkarte. Marysia's forgery apparently stood the test very well: the German gave my card back without a word after turning it over and over and staring at it. Then he examined my Arbeitskarte. I told him a story that was partially true: I was from Warsaw—which fit the documents—from the Todt organization; I intended to report to the Todt branch in Krakow the next day.[82] In the end I convinced him. I can't possibly describe what I went through during that half-hour in the Gestapo station. Even after coming out I wasn't sure I had been released, and I kept looking back over my shoulder to prove I was really free.

Krakow, the capital of the Generalgouvernement, was swarming with Germans. The language spoken in the streets was German. Especially at that time—late 1944—I had the feeling that Gestapo agents were everywhere, watching for "undesirable elements."

One day Marysia—the one we called "Green Marysia" (now Luba Gewisser)—came to my apartment and pleaded with me to go with her to Warsaw to get the ZOB members out. Zivia, Antek, Tuvia, Marek Edelman, and others who had moved from the Old City to Zolibórz were stuck there even after the suppression of the Polish Uprising and the surrender of Tadeusz Bór-Komorowski, the Polish commander.[83]

Brwinów—Grodzisk

That very day I went with Luba to the area around Warsaw, to a town named Grodzisk. There she told me that when she had made her way to me in Krakow, our people were taken

82. The Todt organization was a semimilitary governmental unit established in 1938 for military construction. It was administered by Dr. Fritz Todt until his death in 1942, and later by Albert Speer.

83. Tadeusz Bór-Komorowski was deputy commander of the AK. After Grot-Rowecki fell, he took command and led the Polish Uprising of 1944. He died in exile in 1966 at age 71.

from their hideout to the hospital in Brwinów (a neighborhood on the outskirts of Warsaw). They told Luba that the
move had been initiated by a woman named Amalia, who
had negotiated with the director of the hospital. He had suggested "absorbing" Marek, Zivia, Antek, and Tuvia as "pa-
tients." Accordingly, in collusion with the director, they
were admitted to the hospital. At a checkpoint on the way
there, a suspicious German wanted to take off Marek's bandage. One of the escorts kept her presence of mind and started
shouting, "Typhus! Typhus!" at which the German re-
coiled.[84]

Because I was the only one in the group who looked Aryan,
I was asked to join them in the hospital, to serve as a cover
for their Polishness. Even though I was still angry and bitter
over the Leszno affair, I felt obliged to give in and became a
"patient" for about two weeks for their sake.

One of the nurses was in on the secret, and only after the
war did I learn that she was a Jew. She instructed me about
what to say to the doctor on duty during the examination. I
pretended to be sick. The doctor pressed and poked, and I
responded with a moan to every pressure. Finally, he decided
I was "sick enough" to remain hospitalized. I shared a room
with Marek. Zivia was in the next room. The nurse used to
take our temperatures and such. It wasn't hard, since I didn't
have to pretend with her. On Sunday a Catholic priest came
to the hospital for prayers. As the youngest one in the group,
I was asked to assist him. All my cunning tricks to evade that
duty were of no avail, so I served as an altar boy for the Sunday mass. After a hiding place was found for the comrades to
live in, they were taken out of the hospital one by one to the
new residence in Grodzisk; I was the last to leave.

After finishing my role in the hospital, I went to Krakow

84. See also Zuckerman's account of this incident (1993: 553–
555).

to get Irka. There I renewed contact with Zegota and Marysia Marianska. A few days later Marysia told me we that had to get out of the apartment fast because there was good reason to fear that the Gestapo was on our trail. Irka and I left at once. Later I learned that the Gestapo were in fact looking for us that night. The Polish underground had double agents—members of the underground recruited by the Gestapo—and the warning might have come from such a person. In any case, we didn't stop to ask questions, investigate, or consider: Irka and I simply took off and went to Grodzisk, where we were together again with our friends.

9 Conclusions: Mission to Lublin

This was about the end of December 1944, or perhaps the beginning of January 1945. Contact between the ZOB and the AL was reestablished, and Irka and I were assigned to try to get through to Lublin, where the Provisional Polish Government was already in operation.[85] In mid-January 1945 we set out for Pjaseczno, which, according to our information, was close to the front. When we got to the town, we tried to explore the area and to collect vital information about the Russians' location. It took two or three days to carry out this complicated mission. We decided to cross the lines to the Red Army at night. At dusk the Soviets launched an air raid. We saw German soldiers who looked gloomy but still maintained perfect order, marching in formation. Rumors circulated in the town that the Germans were withdrawing, that they were mining key points and intended to blow them up during the night.

After midnight we left the town for the front lines. Throughout the war a curfew was in effect, and it was forbidden to be outside. We ran from house to house. In one of the courtyards we heard voices speaking a strange language— neither German nor Polish. We hid, pricking up our ears in an attempt to understand. Darkness prevailed, but I could make out that the tanks passing by weren't German. We went into the street and came on someone who said, "The Russians are here!" We couldn't believe our ears, but he insisted it was true. "Sir, at such a time, are you in a mood to joke with us?" I asked. He replied, "I'm not joking. Come and see for yourself." We went with him and soon discovered with our own eyes that the Russians had arrived.

85. Lublin was liberated by the Red Army and served as the temporary capital for the Soviet-supported Polish government.

Following our instructions, we asked the first officer we met to take us to the district commander of the front. Our request was granted. We were introduced to the commander, a brigadier general. He was indeed the very officer we had been sent to meet. We gave the password and, after a brief interrogation, he promised to send us to Lublin. We were supposed to report to Gomulka, whose name I been given by the AL.[86] Early the next morning we boarded a freight train that was also carrying prisoners of war—SS men—to a prison camp near Lublin. That very night we reported to Gomulka in Lublin. We introduced ourselves and said we had been sent by the AL; we spelled out our requests—essentially, the quick liberation of the area where the remnants of the AL and their headquarters were. Gomulka explained that he wasn't sure it was possible at that stage. "Anyway," he said, "the front is moving forward quickly. In another few days, the entire area will be conquered by the Polish-Russian army."

In Gomulka's big office, we talked freely about the situation of the Jews in prewar Poland, and about what was desirable and expected after the war. Gomulka stated his opinion that the Jews had to increase their proportion in the productive professions. When the conversation was over, he invited us to go with him to the central building of the Polish Communist party in Lublin. On the way, he asked whom we knew. When we got to the party building, we realized that we had been invited there as a further test of our reliability.. We met people whose names we had mentioned in our conversation with Gomulka. Immediately we felt a change in the way we were treated, even by Gomulka himself: the at-

86. Wladyslaw Gomulka (1905–1982), a major figure in postwar Polish politics, was the First Secretary of the Polish Communist party from 1956 to 1970.

mosphere became warmer and friendlier. Instructions were given to find us a place to spend the night, and they continued to take care of us in the following days.

The next day we met with Sommerstein, who had been a member of the Polish Sejm before the war and was imprisoned in the Soviet Union during the war.[87] When the Provisional Polish Government was formed, the Soviets came into his prison and ordered, "Sommerstein, you're a minister!" When I asked how it was in prison, he answered in Yiddish, "Honig hob ikh dort nit gelekt" (I didn't lick honey there).

On the day Warsaw was liberated, January 17, 1945, we were still in Lublin on the AL mission, looking for a way to return to Warsaw. I also had personal reasons to go back: I wanted to find out what had happened to my parents and my sister. We were accompanied to the train carrying the chief rabbi of the Polish army, Rabbi Kahane, and we traveled to Warsaw with him.

The War Ends, but Not the Accounting

I was back in Warsaw.

The city was steeped in utter gloom. About 90 percent of the houses were destroyed. There were piles of rubble wherever you looked. The wind blew harder than before, whipping and making me shiver. I was standing on the ruins of my hometown. The wind carried the smell of dead bodies to my

---

87. The Sejm is the Polish parliament. Emil Sommerstein (1883–1957), the Zionist leader, was born in Hleszczawa, Tarnopol District. He spent the war in a Soviet prison and was released in 1944, when he returned to Poland with the Red Army. Appointed to the Polish Committee for National Liberation in July 1944, he moved to Lublin in February 1945. In April 1946 he went to the United States with a delegation of Polish Jews; he fell ill there and stayed. He died in New York.

nose. An awful emptiness, as if Irka and I were the only living souls in the entire city. Something froze in me. I might have gone on standing like that, stuck to the spot, like one of the heaps of debris, if not for a passing Soviet patrol. Two Red Army soldiers stopped us. Thanks to them, my sense of Warsaw returned, commanding me to be always alert and tense. If you loved life, you couldn't give in to paralysis lest you'd fall into a trap. The first thing the victors did was to search us. And to begin with they took my wristwatch and the little bit of money in my pocket. I was aghast: was this how my liberators would treat me? I flew into a rage, but I immediately understood from their looks that they were liable to kill me, just like that. They took all we had and went off. I was furious, but I didn't give in. I hurried to the nearest police station and found myself standing before a locked iron gate. I pounded on the gate with my fists, and on the other side a sleepy guard appeared and asked what I wanted. I explained and asked for his help. He replied with obvious reluctance. Faced with his indifference, I pulled out my "secret weapon": with a meaningful wink, I told the guard that I was an important member of the underground and that I wouldn't "let this pass in silence." My request was granted. About ten police were sent to locate the Soviet patrol and, after a short scouting mission, a group of soldiers was arrested. We were taken together to the police station, where, in the lamplight, I discovered that our robbers weren't among them. I came out of the whole thing disgracefully.

Afterward, I went to the house where I had lived with my parents before the family was moved to the Ghetto. I supposed that, if my parents were still alive, it was reasonable to assume they would return here. I didn't find anyone. Tenants and neighbors hadn't even heard anything about them.

The next day I went to the office responsible for distributing apartments to residents of the city and introduced myself to the official. After some discussion, I convinced him that I was entitled to a spacious apartment, "one of the biggest intact apartments in this city." I pressed, I spoke authoritatively, and in the end I got an apartment on Aleje Jerozolimska (Jerusalem Boulevard) in an apartment house that had miraculously escaped destruction. It was indeed a large apartment, better than the one we had had before the war. I moved in and started searching for my parents. By that time, a Jewish committee existed in Praga to take care of surviving Jews. They also kept a list of returning Jews and operated a Department for Searching for Relatives, through which I finally succeeded in getting in touch with my parents.

Let me go back a bit: I had always been worried about my parents, even before the liberation of Warsaw, but I didn't know how to find out what had happened to them or how to contact them. After the Polish Uprising, when I was still in Grodzisk, I tried to search for them. I got hold of the appropriate papers, put on rustic clothes, boots, and a brushed coat, and went to the area around the village of Siekierki, where a peasant family had sheltered them in exchange for maintenance expenses. I walked around for several days. Whole populations were uprooted, and a person looking for his relatives was not a rare sight.

I discovered the peasant family and dropped in on them. They looked at me like a creature from another world. I began by politely asking how they were, but I couldn't conceal my burning concern. "Where are my parents?" I blurted out the question, along with its implicit threat. The peasants answered that they didn't know exactly, but that my father was someplace not far away. "It's 100 percent certain he's survived," they said, adding that they thought he was working for Germans and was registered under a Polish name. Sensing that they were hiding something from me, I nearly went out of my mind. I cursed and shouted and even pointed my gun at them, threatening to kill them if they didn't tell me the truth at once. I hinted that the house was surrounded by my comrades. I didn't buy the peasants' story because my father looked very Semitic; but I did believe them when they said that my mother was hiding as a Christian with some peasants, although they didn't know where. Despite my pleas and threats, the peasants stuck to their story, assuring me over and over again that everything they said was true.

I stayed with the peasants a long time. I decided to go on searching for my parents with the fragments of information I had collected. It was a hard and complicated task, because I didn't know what names my parents had chosen for themselves. Every suspicious question could bring a catastrophe down on their heads. I wandered around the area for a few days, trying not to be conspicuous or suspicious, but came up with nothing. In my heart, I believed that my mother was still alive, but not my father.

While searching and wandering around the villages in the area, I was stopped by a German reconnaissance unit and asked what I was doing. Naturally, they didn't suspect I was a Jew. I had a forester's document and pulled it out with a contemptuous gesture. The patrol saluted me and left, and I went on my way. In those days, a forester was thought to be close to the powers that be, a collaborator, reporting to the Germans on what was done in the forest, and especially giving information about underground members.

The search for my parents was really the only "vacation" I took during all those years. I returned to Grodzisk and later, through the Department for Searching for Relatives, found my parents and took them to the apartment I had prepared for them in Warsaw.

From my mother and father, I learned that the Gentiles in Siekierki had been telling the truth. After the civilian population was expelled from Warsaw, when the Polish Uprising was crushed, the Germans took my parents and other people outside the city and left them there. Because of his looks, my father decided to put a bandage over half his face, covering one of his eyes to make himself look "more Christian." He also pretended to be mute and feeble-minded. Thus, he went with a group of German cavalry and became their groom, cleaning the stables and horses in exchange for food. And so he lived with the horses until his liberation by the Red Army.

My mother found shelter with a peasant family. She was fluent in Polish and could pass as a Pole. She had no trouble getting along with people, especially peasants, because she had spent most of her life in a village. Her benefactors were convinced they had a pure-bred Polish woman and a pious Christian in their homes. My father and mother didn't know anything about each other. They also found each other through the Department for Searching for Relatives in Praga.

We were one of the few happy Jewish families who remained almost whole after the war, though my brother and sister had been killed. It was rare that parents and some of their children survived. Although we had hoped for liberation all through the war, it caught us by surprise and there was no joy in our hearts. Only then, it seems to me, did we begin to grasp the magnitude of the catastrophe that had befallen the Jewish people and our own family.

We didn't know where to begin: to return to our prewar life was impossible, if only for the simple reason that our former apartment was occupied by a Polish family, and we didn't intend to fight for our property or our rights. From the start, we saw our stay in Warsaw as temporary. Clearly, at the first opportunity we would get up and go. Although we had a big family in Argentina—father had brothers and sisters who had been there for many years and were quite well off— it never occurred to us to immigrate there. We had no doubt that we would go to Eretz Israel.

My fighting companions at that time were busy restoring the movement, in Brikha and Aliya B.[88] Through my connec-

88. Brikha and Aliya B were organized to get Jewish immigrants

tions in the housing office, I helped obtain another apartment in our building on Poznanska Street, which was intended as a base for Brikha. The people who came through there lived in a commune until they left for Eretz Israel.

Interim Stops

In February 1945, I set out with a few friends. Passing through Czechoslovakia and Romania, I stopped in Bucharest, where Brikha bases had been set up. I stayed on Vitoro Levi Street, where I met Abba Kovner and his wife, Vitka.[89] I myself did not regard immigration to Israel as the first priority. I thought we still had something to do in Europe: to settle our account with the Germans.[90] On this point I found a common language with Vitka and Abba Kovner, but when I tried to bring the subject up with Zivia, who also came to Bucharest about that time, I saw that she didn't share my opinion. She

---

out of postwar Europe and smuggle them illegally into Eretz Israel under the British Mandate.

89. Abba Kovner (1918–1987) was the leader of Ha-Shomer Ha-Za'ir in Vilna, commander of the United Partisan Organization (FPO) in the Vilna Ghetto (after the death of Itsik Wittenberg), and partisan leader in Rudnicka Forest. After immigrating to Israel, he became a Hebrew poet and designer of the Diaspora Museum in Tel Aviv.

Vitka Kempner-Kovner was a partisan and member of the FPO in Vilna. In May 1942, she and two others blew up a German troop train headed for the front. In October 1943, from their base in Rudnicka Forest, she walked 25 kilometers to Vilna with a suitcase of explosives, blew up the power plant, and rescued 60 Jews from Kailis Camp. She married Abba Kovner and now lives in Israel.

90. This refers to a group formed by Abba Kovner to wreak vengeance on the Germans for the Holocaust; as yet there is no full account of their activities. The only published work about the organization is an article by Levi Arye Sarid (1992).

thought we should immigrate to Eretz Israel as soon as possible. So our paths diverged.

To camouflage my future activities in Germany, Abba Kovner and I agreed that I would return to Poland and leave from there again, this time for Italy. In Poland I went to the members of Brikha and offered my help smuggling people across the border. I was assigned to lead forty to fifty people through Czechoslovakia to Hungary. At that time—before the German surrender—Europe was experiencing a migration of peoples. Nevertheless, the Czech-Polish border was guarded on both sides and whoever wanted to pass had to identify himself and explain his purpose. We approached the border in the evening. I had planned to cross into Czechoslovakia at dark. There were old people and children in the group who couldn't maintain absolute silence. We were quickly stopped by Polish soldiers and taken to the guard station. In the interrogation, I showed them the document of a representative of the International Red Cross and presented the group as Hungarians returning home. I pretended I didn't know Polish. They searched members of the group thoroughly and confiscated whatever valuables they found. This infuriated me. I shouted and banged on the table, overturning an inkwell and spilling ink all over. I heard the soldiers whispering to one another to take me outside and "finish me off." I demanded that they take me to the commander, and they agreed. I explained to him that his soldiers were behaving dishonorably—that these were people who had been uprooted by the Germans and wanted to return home. "Is such behavior possible!" I protested. To appease us, even if only a little, the commander promised that an escort of soldiers would put us on the train before dawn and tell the Czech soldiers we had already passed through the checkpoint. This is indeed what happened.

At the Brikha crossing point, I left the group and continued on alone. I didn't take my parents with me—they stayed in

Poland. After I realized I would stay in Europe for some time before immigrating to Eretz Israel, I requested that they be allowed to go there on their own. They were taken with a group of immigrants to Italy, where they waited their turn to immigrate legally to Eretz Israel. After about two and a half years, they arrived in Eretz Israel in November 1947, just before the UN accepted the Partition Plan.[91] I got there before them, having immigrated to Eretz Israel illegally with Aliya B on the Hagana ship *Biriya*. I was in the last group of illegal immigrants imprisoned in the internment camp of Atlit, the last group arrested in the domain of Eretz Israel.[92] Later, camps were opened in Cyprus. After staying in Atlit for a few weeks, we were released in June 1946. I was a free man in Eretz Israel.

Epilogue

A harsh and disappointing reality awaited me in Eretz Israel.

My meeting with Melekh Neustadt, one of the first people I met here, concerned the fighters of the Warsaw Ghetto. I was interrogated about everyone who had been killed, but I was never asked, even remotely, about those who had survived.

In almost every meeting with people in Eretz Israel, the question came up, "How did you survive?" It was asked again and again, and not always in the most delicate way. I had the feeling that I was guilty for surviving. This was why, even after I learned Hebrew, I didn't talk very much. I avoided

91. The Partition Plan, under which Palestine would be divided into an Arab and a Jewish state, was accepted by the UN on Nov. 19, 1947. The plan was accepted by the Jews but rejected by the Arabs. The British declared that they would do nothing to enforce it.

92. Atlit was a British internment camp for illegal Jewish immigrants near Haifa.

exposing my past. I preferred not to tell about myself and where I had spent the war years.

To this day, I am grateful to Zippora Chizik, who served as director of the Absorption Department in the Labor Committee of Tel Aviv. She took care of me loyally and devotedly, and even let me live in her home for a few months. She had two sons, one my age and one older, both already out of the house. At the time, I wasn't aware of the problems I caused. Her husband later told me that every night, the entire time I stayed in their house, I would scream horribly in my sleep and awaken him and Zippora. Yet they gave me a home until I got on my feet and moved to an apartment I rented from an Arab in the village of Somayl. Zippora helped me find work. At my explicit request, it was not clerical work but physical labor, in construction.

In those days, I felt an internal need for physical labor. It soothed me. After a day's work in construction, I would come home exhausted but calmer. Theoretically, one period of my life was over and a new one had begun, in our ancestral homeland. In fact, that time of my life is an inseparable part of me to this day, an axis my little world revolves around. The experience is still happening, still going on.

Appendix: Journal of a Fighter

The following account of the Warsaw Ghetto Uprising was written by Kazik and sent clandestinely from Warsaw on May 24, 1944. I have tried to retain the original sequence of tenses as far as possible.

1. Defense of the Brushmakers' Area

On the first day, April 18 (1943), at midnight, we were suddenly awakened by the alarm bell at the observation post. We all leaped up. We dressed quickly and took up our positions: we were a fighting group commanded by Hanoch Gutman, on Walowa Street 6. Our group included Zvi Edelstein,[1] Shlomek (Shlomo) Shuster, Dvora Baran, Zippora Lerer,[2] Faytshe (Zippora) Rabov,[3] Adolf Hochberg, Yosef Oberstein,[4] Yasin-

---

1. Zvi Edelstein (1922–1943), born in Warsaw, was active in the Zionist youth movement. He escaped to the Aryan side of Warsaw, where he was captured and killed by the Germans on May 6, 1943.

2. Zippora Lerer (1920–1943), born in Volyn, was active in the Zionist youth movement and in the Ghetto underground. She worked in Janusz Korczak's orphanage and died in battle on May 3, 1943.

3. Faytshe (Zippora) Rabov (1921–1943), born in the Bialystok district, was active in the Zionist youth movement. She came from Lódz to Warsaw at the outbreak of the war and was active in the Ghetto underground. She refused to leave the Ghetto because she wanted to stay with her boyfriend, Hanoch Gutman, who had been wounded. After May 10, 1943, she remained in the Central Ghetto with the remnants of the fighters, who held out for several weeks even though they were isolated from the world.

4. Yosef Oberstein, born in Lódz, moved to Warsaw at the outbreak of the war. He escaped to the Aryan side of the city after the Uprising and was killed in partisan fighting at age 20.

ski (Leyb),[5] Batya Silman,[6] Shlomek (Shlomo) Alterman,[7] Abraham Eiger, and me. Thus what we were ready for, came. The Brushmakers' Area was surrounded by gendarmes and Ukrainian mercenaries. I stood on the balcony facing Walowa Street. Beyond the wall, Germans and Ukrainians were seen, shooting at our windows from time to time, for no good reason, for fun. We got an order not to annoy them.

At 4 in the morning, we saw at the Nalewki Passage a line of Nazis marching to the Central Ghetto. They walked and walked endlessly. There were a few thousand of them. They were followed by a procession of tanks, armored vehicles, light cannons, and a few hundred Waffen SS on motorcycles. "They're going as to war," I said to my companion at the post, Zippora (Lerer); and suddenly I felt how very weak we were. What were we and what was our strength against an armed and well-equipped army, against tanks and armored vehicles, while we had only pistols and, at most, grenades? But our spirit didn't flag. Here we were waiting to settle accounts with our executioners at last. The rumble of machine gun fire, the explosion of grenades, and the echo of rifle bullets reached us from the Central Ghetto. We distinguished between the shots: that's a German one and that's ours. Here's our mine, our grenade. In our area, the day passed quietly. At dusk came Többens's letter calling on everyone to come to

5. Leyb Yasinski, born in Warsaw, was active in the Zionist youth movement. He was killed in the escape from the sewers on May 10, 1943, at age 23.

6. Batya Silman was an active member of the Zionist youth movement. She refused to leave the Ghetto to join her mother on the Aryan side of Warsaw and fell in the Uprising in May 1943, at age 18.

7. Shlomek Alterman (1919–1943) grew up in Warsaw and was active in the Zionist youth movement. He worked with war refugees in Warsaw, built the ZOB bunkers on Ogrodowa and Zamenhof streets, and was killed in the Uprising.

work, since there would be no aktsia in the Brushmakers' Area.[8] At sunset we abandoned our positions, left scouts in the observation post, and went to the living quarters of the unit. Here we remained in a state of readiness for several days; indeed today the situation is excellent. Everyone held onto his weapons and the equipment he was given.

2. Third Day (April 20, first day of Passover 1943)

Three in the afternoon. I am on guard at the observation post with the switch to activate the mine. A unit of about 300 Germans coming from Franciszkanska Street turns into Walowa Street, into our area. In a flash I grab the switch with one hand and press the alarm bell with the other. The commander bursts in on me: the Germans are approaching. They're at the gate. Suddenly there's a tremendous explosion: I see bodies flying, arms and legs cut off. Eighty to a hundred killed are lying in the streets. The rest of the Germans retreat in a panic.[9] Meanwhile, we take up our posi-

8. Walter Caspar Többens was one of the major German employers in the Warsaw Ghetto. His factories produced military uniforms. In November 1946 he escaped from a train extraditing him to Poland to be tried for war crimes. He was tried in absentia in Bremen in 1949 and sentenced to ten years in a labor camp. In his report of April 20, 1943, Nazi General Jürgen Stroop states: "I prevailed on the firms W. C. Többens, Shultz & Co., and Hoffmann to be ready for evacuation with their entire personnel on 21 April 1943 at 0600 hours, so we can at last see our way toward purging the Ghetto. The trustee for Többens pledged to lead the 4,000 to 5,000 Jews on a voluntary basis to the designated assembly point for the move" (Stroop 1979). Also see Gutman 1989: 383–386.

9. The mine was prepared by Michal Klepfisz two months before the outbreak of the battles; it was planted by a Gordonia unit commanded by Eliezer Geller, a No'ar Ha-Tsioni unit commanded by Yakov Praszkar, and other fighters. Heniek Kleinweiss was especially outstanding in this work.

tions. We wait. One hour goes by, two hours. The Germans assemble, consult, a few high-ranking officers come. Suddenly we hear voices at the gate. The Germans are coming into the courtyard. They are walking in single file, their faces scared and their rifles ready. They aren't walking but running near the walls. My companions and I let the first group of six pass because we don't want to waste a grenade on such a small group. After them, an entire outfit bursts in. We have two homemade grenades, ten Molotov cocktails, and pistols. "Shlomek, light it," I call to my companion Shlomo Shuster, and toss the grenade into the outfit. Explosion. . . . A few fall. We hurl Molotov cocktails and a few Germans catch fire. A hail of bullets pours down on us. We don't want to waste the only grenade we have, and we retreat up the street and take up positions with the rest of the fighters. Everything immediately falls silent. The Germans run away. Half an hour later, they come back. Once again we greet them with Molotov cocktails and grenades. Under heavy fire cover, the Germans retreat, leaving a lot of killed and wounded. One of the Germans sees one of our girls at her post. "Hans, look, a woman," he calls to his companion, and they begin shooting at her; but she doesn't flinch. She greets them properly.[10] One of our fighters, who took up a position in the attic, rains shots down on the soldiers at the walls. Despite the heavy fire of the Germans, he kills six of them. In the courtyard of Swietojerska 32—Walowa 6, one of the directors of the Brushmakers' company, Dr. Laus, appears with two Germans in uniform, waving rifles as a sign that they mean peace. Dr. Laus calls to the fighting organization to dismantle its weapons within 15 minutes. We reply with shots. One of the Germans is killed, Dr. Laus flees. The real siege begins.

10. This refers to Zippora Lerer.

3. The Siege

Cannons roar. Machine guns and mortars rumble. Bullets rain down. All of us are standing at our positions, and the enemy isn't here. We're in despair, there's nobody to fight against. The Germans have taken up positions outside the walls and pour a hail of bullets and grenades down on us. Suddenly, flames surrounded our house; because of the flames and the stifling smoke, we are forced to abandon our positions. Three men cover the retreat; we withdraw to the shelter at Swietojerska 34.[11] This is the concentration point for all the active groups in the Brushmakers' Area. We find one group there. Two groups are missing. The two remaining groups begin gathering and I am appointed commander of the guard. I immediately set men on guard—even though that wasn't necessary, because people volunteered on their own—and we went out to find our companions. On the way, we collided with the Germans but didn't succeed in fighting with them. A few times we tried to make contact with those groups, but without any result. At 11 at night, three of us went out: the commander of the Brushmakers' Area, Marek Edelman; the commander of my group, Heniek (Hanoch) Gutman; and I. In the attic, we found the body of our companion Michal Klepfisz, who had been hit by submachine gun bullets.[12] We examined him but didn't find his pistol. The Germans almost certainly took it. We went on walking and came on a guard of two of our groups who were also looking for us. We brought them all into the shelter at Swietojerska

11. This underground shelter was built by the Jewish Fighting Organization a few months before the beginning of the battles.

12. Michal Klepfisz, born in Warsaw, was an engineer and an active Bundist. He was instrumental in obtaining weapons and the formula for Molotov cocktails. He fought in the April Uprising and died at the age of about 30.

34. The residents of the shelter greeted them very warmly. Everyone appealed to us to take them into the Fighting Organization. Unfortunately, we didn't even have enough weapons for all the fighters. All of them were thirsty for battle. The echo of grenades exploding reached our ears, along with the incessant crack of machine gun fire. All night long we were busy cleaning our weapons, checking homemade bullets and grenade wicks, and finally we got a little rest.

4. Fourth Day (April 21, second day of Passover)

All day long guards of the Jewish Fighting Organization walk around the whole area and the Germans aren't seen. At dusk people stream to us from the whole area. Their shelters were burned down, and some people were burned alive. The whole area is surrounded by flames. We decided to get through to the Central Ghetto. A meeting. We lined up and went out of the yard. As long as I live I'll never forget that picture. The night is dark, but here—broad daylight, an explosion of walls and houses burning down. We are surrounded by flames. We pass through burning shops. An indescribable heat comes from all around. The glass is melting all over the yard. We run in single file through the yard, with wet handkerchiefs on our faces. At last we broke a way through to the yard at Franciszkanska 21. Our objective: to get to the house at Franciszkanska 20. We only had to cross the street, apparently a very simple thing. But I must state that the wall along Bonifraterska Street was destroyed. At the junction with Franciszkanska Street, the wall separating the Brushmakers' Area and no-man's-land was also destroyed, and between them lurked guards of Latvians, Ukraininans, Germans, and the blue police.[13] One group tries to get through. They come back and announce that machine guns are set up in the destroyed

13. I.e., Polish police.

places; because of that, the commanders decided to disperse the groups. (Yakov) Praszker's[14] group returns to the Brushmakers' Area, and we are assigned to break through. (Hanoch) Gutman's group leads. We divide into two groups of five; those who go on the reconnaissance mission are Shlomek (Shlomo Shuster) and I. Shlomo stays in front of the gate; I sneak to the destroyed wall, look around alertly, give him the signal—and the first group of five crossed safely. I wait a few minutes, give another signal—the second group of five crosses, and I follow them. Then other groups cross, Marek's (Edelman) and Berlinski's (Hirsh).[15] The Ghetto looks about like the Brushmakers' Area. We went to the shelter of the supply establishment at Franciszkanska Street 30.[16]

5. Fifth Day (April 22) and the Following

We rested throughout the fifth day. That night, before dawn of the sixth day, the guard went to make contact with the active groups in the Central Ghetto. Two people went toward Gesia Street. Yurek (Blonas)[17] and I turned to Nalewki. The

14. Yakov Praszker, born in Lódz, moved to Warsaw after the outbreak of the war and became a trusted and admired member of the underground. He commanded a fighting unit of Zionist youth and fell in the April Uprising.

15. Hirsh Berlinski (1908–1944), born in Lódz, was active in the underground movement and represented Po'alei Zion Left on the ZOB command staff. He fought in the April Uprising and escaped through the sewers to the Aryan side. He was killed in the Polish Uprising.

16. These were the supply warehouses run by Abraham Gepner, where the fighters were always greeted warmly and helped as much as possible.

17. Yurek Blonas, born in Warsaw, was a Bundist from an early age. He was 15 when the war broke out and was active in the Ghetto underground, smuggling weapons. He was a commander of the Bund unit in the Brushmakers' Area. He escaped through the sewers on

street was full of dead bodies. To avoid trampling on them, we jumped from place to place. At Nalewki 36 we came on a fighting group commanded by Lutek (Leyb) Rotblat. From that moment on we have constant contact with the headquarters of the Fighting Organization and with all the groups. There aren't any serious actions except for skirmishes with the guards. Three days later, we were forced to leave the shelter of the supply establishment, which served as a center for sorties. We moved to no-man's-land. But there too we were forced to leave the shelter because of the flames and the choking smoke. The situation in the shelters is desperate and hopeless. Most palpable is the lack of air, water, and food. Day after day passes. On the tenth day after the aktsia, the Ghetto is burned. Everywhere—sooty bodies. In the streets, in the courtyards, and in the cellars, people are burned alive. Because of this dreadful situation and the inability to continue the war because of (1) a lack of equipment, (2) a lack of food and water, and (3) the impossibility of engaging the enemy in battle—since he is not within the Ghetto but is destroying the Ghetto from outside—we are forced to accept the idea of getting our people out to the forest to continue with our war.

6. We Seek Contacts with the Aryan Side

On April 29 (Thursday), the command staff, which included Mordechai (Anielewicz), Zivia Lubetkin, Marek (Edelman), Michal (Rosenfeld),[18] and Berlinski (Hirsh), decided to send

---

May 8 but was killed along with Shlomo Shuster when they went on a failed attempt to lead other fighters to safety.

18. Michal Rosenfeld, a graduate of Warsaw University, was a member of the ZOB command staff. He fought in the Central Ghetto and escaped through the sewers. He was killed in a clash with the Germans and was about 30 when he died.

Zygmunt (Fryderych) and me to make contact with the commander of the Jewish Fighting Organization on the Aryan side, Antek (pseudonym of Yitzhak Zuckerman). On the night of April 29 we set out for Muranowska Street, and from there we passed through a tunnel to the Aryan side, accompanied by Adolf (Hochberg) and Lolek.[19] We parted from our companions and went up to the attic to wait for morning. In the morning, we looked around and saw bodies on the neighboring roofs. We went to the courtyard: the window panes were exploded, all around were heaps of rifle and pistol bullet casings. We have the impression that the house is empty. We have no idea where we are. We decided to go out and peep into the street. Suddenly we met a trolley car driver, a Pole. From a conversation with him, we learn that 60 Jews were discovered hiding in this house. Impossible to go out. We

19. Lolek was a young fighter, about 19 years old. A member of the Communist Youth, he joined Ha-Shomer Ha-Tza'ir during the war. We have not succeeded in identifying him.

During the battles, other emissaries were also sent from the Central Ghetto to the Aryan side to make contact with representatives of the Jewish Fighting Organization and to hasten help. On May 7 a delegation of 11 fighters was assigned to break a path to the Aryan side. The delegation included Aharon Bruskin (Pavel), Yitzhak Sukenik (Koza), Wanda Okhron, Lilka Jimak, Siegfrieda Simson, and Hela Schüpper. After many adventures, the group came through the tunnel to a place on the Aryan side, across from Krasinski Park, but a few of them perished in conflicts with the Polish and German police. That night, another delegation was sent, consisting of Tuvia Borzykowski, Israel Kanal, Mordechai Growas, Menachem Bigelman, and six more fighters. On the way, they came upon Germans. A battle began in which a few Germans fell. Seven of the fighters, including four who were wounded, managed to break through back to the fighting positions; three of them who didn't succeed remained in a struggle all night with vastly superior German forces.

started telling him made-up stories, that we had gone to the Ghetto on Sunday night to bring old clothes and had got stuck there, and now we had managed to get out. The driver started congratulating us, assured us that we would have material for a whole book. He showed us a hole where you could go through to Sierakowska Street, and we made it out safely.

In the street, we recognized a *Shmaltsovnik* (blackmailer) who was following us. But we fled right under his nose. That day we made contact with Antek (Yitzhak Zuckerman), with the courier Franya Beatus, and with Tadek (Tuvia Shayngut). We gave him (Antek) a report on the situation in the Ghetto and explained the issue of helping. As I learned, we couldn't expect any help. We were doomed to act on our own. Every one of us was therefore asked to increase contacts. Those who showed up to cooperate were Stefan (Sawicki), Kostek (Krzaczek),[20] Anna (Wachalska), Stefan P. (Pokropek). Their help was decisive for us and we are grateful for it. After running around for a few days, we managed to contact "smugglers" on Kozla Street. They were to make it easier for us to go down to the tunnel. But at the last minute—they refused. We remained in the street after curfew, without a place to spend the night. Finally, after 8 days, Kostek found a sewer worker.

20. Kostek was a member of the PPR, the Communist movement. A Pole who worked under the name of Krzaczek, he was called Kostek in writing so that those who transmitted the report—members of the Polish underground of the Government-in-Exile in London—would not know about the cooperation of the Communists. He also helped members of the Jewish underground in many other incidents. In early 1944, when Yakov Faygenblat, Guta Kwonki, and Zygmunt Igla were killed in hiding on Prozna Street 14, Krzaczek went to the Gestapo offices equipped with a forged document of a Nazi party member to find out the reason for the failure of the operation. He did not succeed and lost his life.

7. Delegation to the Ghetto

On Thursday night, the eve of May 8, a delegation composed of Ryszek and two sewer workers set out for the Ghetto. It failed and had to return. The next day another delegation was formed. The two sewer workers walked, followed by Ryszek and me. Tadek and Kostek stayed above ground. I should add that, for the success of the delegation, we had to make contact with the King of the Shmaltsovniks and his assistants in Kazimierz Square. On the night before May 9, at 10:30, we descended to the sewer. The sewer workers led the way and I walked behind them. When we had gone a few dozen meters, they stood still and announced that they wouldn't go on. They were as drunk as Lot. I said in an authoritative tone, "You're under my command. Forward march!" I cannot describe how we walked with them. Every hundred yards they stood still and demanded brandy, kvas, and food.[21] No coaxing helped. Only my gun influenced them. I came out of the sewer at two in the morning, at the corner of Stawki and Zamenhof streets. Ryszek stayed with the sewer workers. Zamenhof Street was lighted with a searchlight from Dzika Street. I had to crawl on my belly to Muranowska Street. I had some addresses of our fighting groups. First I went to the shelter of the supply institution at Franciszkanska 30. I left the shelter when I went out to the Aryan side. I entered the courtyard but found only ruins of the shelter. Apparently the Germans had discovered it. In the second courtyard, among the ruins, I met three people. They didn't look like human beings, but like ghosts. I found two men and a woman in the ruins. The woman was groaning, her leg was broken. I wanted to take them with me to the Aryan side, but they didn't have the strength to stand up. I learned from them that the shelter had been discovered a few days before. The fighters had

21. Kvas is a light beer.

staged a splendid battle, fought against a few dozen Germans. They told me that, as the fighter Abraham Eiger lay wounded, he called to the Germans but they were afraid to get close to him. When his strength ran out and he stopped shooting, the German stabbed him with a bayonet. Shlomek (Shlomo Shuster), even though he was only 17, showed marvelous courage and fought like a lion. He later fell on the Aryan side.

I left those three unfortunates to their fate and went to Franciszkanska 22. I didn't recognize the shelters in that courtyard. I signal with my flashlight and call my companions with the password. Suddenly, from the ruins, a human voice rises, wanting to lead me to the shelter where our companions are. I recognized a woman's voice. She told me her leg was broken and that I should look for her in the heaps of debris. I searched for her for half an hour and didn't find her. I was forced to stop looking. In despair, I hurried to Nalewki Street 33, 35, to Mila Street 19, to Zamenhof 29. But I didn't find anyone anywhere. The Ghetto was burned down to its foundations. Piles of corpses rolled around in the streets, the courtyards, and among the mounds of ruins.

I consider why I am returning. Suddenly I felt good among those ruins and those bodies that were so dear to me. I want to take revenge and perish. But I don't give into my weakness. Duty called me to go back. At 4 o'clock I returned to the sewer. I closed the manhole cover behind me. "Let's go," I shouted in an inhuman voice to Ryszek and the sewer workers; "there's nobody." We began walking back. We were soaked to the skin because all cisterns and sluice gates were closed. The water comes up to our waist. We walk and I signal with my flashlight in the hope that, nevertheless, there would be someone. I shouted, "Jan! Jan!"—the password of the fighters. Suddenly, a group of 10 fighters bursts out of a side channel.[22] Tearfully, we greet one another. In a few

22. These were Shlomek Shuster, Guta, Eliezer and Yurek Blonas,

words I learn everything that had happened during my absence. Help was late in coming. By one day! We had no choice but to save those who remained. Two fighters return to the Ghetto to take those who are left. Meanwhile, we advance slowly toward Prosta Street. We post scouts along the way, a few dozen meters apart. On the way, I talk with Shlomek Shuster and learn these details from him: The shelter at Mila 18 was discovered only on May 8, during the day. Most of our companions committed suicide at the last minute. I understand the act well: hungry, broken, and exhausted, a hopeless situation, without any help. After I gathered the people under the manhole cover of the sewer on Prosta Street, I went out to the Aryan side again, to the Shmaltsovnik, where I had left my clothes when I descended into the sewer. Tadek and Kostek were waiting for me there. I told them the situation as it was. We agreed that the next day, at 5 in the morning, we would take the people out of the sewer and move them to the forest. Kostek was to get hold of trucks. At 5 that evening I went to the manhole cover with Tadek. We got a letter from the fighters that, at 5 in the morning, they would all gather under the manhole cover.

Abrasha Blum, Abraham Stolak, Bronka Manalek, Janek Bielak (a Bundist, technician by training, fell in the Polish Uprising in Warsaw of August–September 1944), Faygele Goldstein (member of the Bund, girlfriend of Yurek Blonas, fell in the village of Plodi along with Zalman Frydrych and three members of the Blonas family), and Pnina Papier (one of those who was rescued and lived in Israel). This was the first group that left for the sewers on the night of May 8 from the shelter at Franciszkanska Street 22. When they met with Kazik in the sewer, two were returned as emissaries to the shelter, and all the fighters who were there went to the sewer. This shelter on Franciszkanska Street also served as a refuge for the fighters who remained in the Ghetto after May 8, 1943. In June 1943 a group of Jewish fighters was said to be poisoned by phosgene gas by the Germans.

8. Monday, May 10

At 5 o'clock in the morning we are at the manhole cover. I am waiting for Tadek and the trucks that Kostek was to get. Half an hour later, Tadek came. We walked around on Prosta Street. An hour went by, two hours—and no Kostek. Our nerves on edge. We decided to get hold of trucks by ourselves.[23] Tadek had some possibilities of getting them. He went and I remained alone. It was 9 in the morning; none of them came back. It was too late to risk bringing our friends out of the sewer. On the other hand, it was clear to me that if we didn't get the people out, they were doomed to death in the sewer. Therefore, I told myself that we had to get them out today whenever we could. How good it would be if we had an armed guard when we brought them up. But, unfortunately, there is no one. Another hour passed. Suddenly a truck arrives. In it are Kostek and other boys who look good: Jurek, Ryszek, and Wacek. We surround the manhole cover with trucks we prepared in advance, for at the corner of Zelazna Street is a German-Ukrainian post—the post of the small Ghetto. We open the manhole cover. They begin coming out of the cistern. I don't recognize anyone, even though I knew them all, for these weren't people, but exhausted ghosts, barely tottering on their feet. A crowd of people gathered around, looked on, and said, "The cats are coming out." Suddenly I noticed that the manhole cover was open and no one was coming out. Kostek was getting nervous, the truck was already full. At that moment a second truck came. I went to Kostek and learned from him that the second truck wasn't ours. "The truck is already full," I told him, "no one else is coming out. What are we waiting for?" I give an order to close the manhole cover and go. In the truck I find out that 15

23. They telephoned a moving company and asked them to send a truck to transport trees. When the truck arrived, they forced the drivers at gunpoint to take the fighters.

people are left in the sewer who were in a side sewer. The exodus from the sewer lasted half an hour. The group of companions who remained were 15 minutes away from the cistern. We decided that the truck would return to them after it moved the group. We went to the woods near X.[24] I stayed behind to bring the companions to the group of fighters from the Többens workshops, who had been brought out two weeks earlier from Ogrodowa Street. Ryszek, Wacek, and Jurek went back to Warsaw in the truck. At dusk, when I saw that they didn't return, I returned to Warsaw. Passing through Bank Square, I saw a group of people. Some premonition touched my heart and I jumped from the tram. I approached. In front of me lay Ryszek, killed, and some distance away from him, Jurek. Later I learned that they had reached Warsaw and gone to Prosta Street, to the cistern. But a post of gendarmes was already standing there. A woman who recognized them turned them in, testifying that they had participated in bringing out the people. Those who were left in the sewer came out of the cistern and fought the gendarmes. A skirmish erupted, and they were all annihilated.

24. I.e., Łomianki.

References

Ainsztein, Ruben, 1974. *Jewish Resistance in Nazi-Occupied Eastern Europe*. New York: Harper & Row.

Borzykowski, Tuvia, 1972. *Between Tumbling Walls*, trans. Mendel Kohansky. Tel Aviv: Beit Lohamei Hagettaot and Hakibbutz Hameuchad Publishing House.

Gutman, Yisrael, 1989. *The Jews of Warsaw, 1939–1943: Ghetto, Underground, Revolt*, trans. Ina Friedman. Bloomington: Indiana University Press.

Krall, Hanna, 1986. *Shielding the Flame*, trans. Joanna Stasinska and Lawrence Wechsler. New York: Holt.

Lubetkin, Zivia, 1981. *In the Days of Destruction and Revolt*, trans. Ishai Tubbin. Tel Aviv: Beit Lohamei Hagettaot, Hakibbutz Hameuchad Publishing House, and Am Oved Publishing House.

Meed, Wladka, 1979. *On Both Sides of the Wall*, trans. Steven Meed. New York: Holocaust Library.

Sarid, Levi Arie, 1992. " 'Revenge' Organization: Its History, Character, and Activities," *Yalkut Moreshet* 52 (Hebrew).

Shulman, Abraham, 1982. *The Case of Hotel Polski*. New York: Holocaust Library.

Stroop, Jürgen, 1979. *The Stroop Report: The Jewish Quarter Is No More*, trans. Sybil Morton. New York: Pantheon.

Szwajger, Adina Blady, 1990. *I Remember Nothing More: The Warsaw Children's Hospital and the Jewish Resistance*, trans. Tasja Darowska and Danusia Stok. London: Collins Harvill.

Ziemian, Joseph, 1977. *The Cigarette Sellers of Three Crosses Square*, trans. Janina David. New York: Avon.

Zuckerman, Yitzhak (Antek), 1993. *A Surplus of Memory: Chronicle of the Warsaw Ghetto Uprising*, trans. Barbara Harshav. Los Angeles: University of California Press.

Index